The Parent Slant

The PARENT SLANT

Chester E. Swor

BROADMAN PRESS
Nashville, Tennessee

Library of Congress Catalog Card Number: 70–151132
Dewey Decimal Classification: 301.43
Printed in the United States of America
5.F71W

Dedication

To my precious mother, who despite widowhood and responsibility for the total care of her six children in an age in which social security and aid to dependent children had not even been envisioned, *made* the time to teach her children well, to inspire them to high dreams and honest effort, to guide them to happy identification with Christ and the church, and to believe with all their hearts the wisdom of Proverbs 22:1: "A good name is rather to be chosen than great riches, and loving favour rather than silver and gold." These gifts of instruction she gave to her children out of a life whose example made valid everything she taught. The efficacy of her life and teaching has enabled me to come through these many years with a minimum of confusion and with conviction and courage with which to battle temptation.

Contents

1. Why This Book? . . . 2

2. Parents and Youth in Crisis . . . 14

3. Home: The Soil and the Climate . . . 24

4. Parents Teaching . . .
   Honesty: As the Crow Flies . . . 39

5. Parents Teaching . . .
   Sex: Gift with a Purpose . . . 50

6. Parents Teaching
   Three Hazards: Drugs, Alcohol, Tobacco . . . 62

7. Discipline: Meaning, Significance, Spirit . . . 76

8. Communication and the Generation Gap . . . 92

9. Because You Asked . . . 108

10. Resource and Book List . . . 124

    Findings of Parent-Youth Survey . . . 134

    Notes . . . 138

1

Why This Book?

So many times since the appearance of *The Teen-Age Slant,* coauthored by Jerry Merriman, I have been asked by parents: "Why don't you do a book for parents? We need help as urgently as do the teen-agers!"

I had been a teen-ager; and remembering the complications of those years, and having worked with teen-agers for most of my adult years, I felt I had a degree of qualification to write for teeners. However, I am not a parent, and, therefore, I have had greater reluctance to undertake a book for parents, lest I appear to be posing as an authority in an area of life in which I have not had actual experience.

Two conversations changed my mind in that regard. First, two parents said to me: "You have not reared children of your own, but you have been a substitute parent many times. Furthermore, young people talk to you more fully and frankly than they talk to their parents generally, and you could be most helpful to those of us who are parents by sharing with us the needs they share with you."

Later, several young people in a high school in which I had spent a week in answering their questions suggested this possibility: "Dr. Swor, why don't you write a book for parents, giving them some of the information which you have given to us? They might listen to you in some instances in which they wouldn't listen to us."

Therefore, though still with some misgivings, I undertook the gathering, sifting, and classification of materials from which, hopefully, a helpful book could grow. I talked with hundreds of parents, many of whom shared their hopes, confusions, frustrations, and frequent victories in dealing with their youngsters. I kept a searching eye for book and magazine materials; I kept a listening ear to all who had something to say about parents and youth. I listened anew to great numbers of teen-agers concerning their problems and needs as related, on one hand, to daily problems and, on the other hand, to their parents.

It became apparent that both parents and their youngsters "have a point" in the misunderstandings which so often widen the understanding gap and alienate them. It became apparent, also, that many parents are doing an excellent job of communicating with their children and of guiding them well through the many shoals of today's youth society, and from them I learned much. Equally apparent was the deepening impression that many young people are on good terms with their parents and are leading happy, well-balanced lives.

Therefore, with the hope that I could become a "moderator" of the ageless parent-child relationship problem, and that I might be able to convey to parents, as I had sought for many years to convey to their children, some of the factors of good family relationships, I undertook the composition of this volume, hoping above all that the book would bring help to the many thousands of sincere, committed parents who want with all their hearts to be good parents. If this book helps a few parents *much* and helps many parents *some,* my efforts will have been rewarded.

In an attempt to derive a fresh report on the *status quo* of parent-teen relationship and rapport, because in the teen years there occurs the greatest test of that relationship and rapport, I sent to 175 teen-agers in 21 different states from Pennsylvania to California and to 175 parent teams questionnaires, asking essentially the same questions of both groups. From the generous returns of those questionnaires I sensed some of the principal needs of both parents and their children in the matter of mutual needs and responsibilities; and, in the light of those needs, I chose the areas which are discussed in this volume. Some highlights of the findings of the questionnaire survey are given here, and the summary of the remainder of the survey may be found in the Addenda section at the conclusion of the book. Many of the written comments of teen-agers and parents will be shared in the various chapters of this volume.

Teen-agers listed these as the main *points of tension* between themselves and their parents:

1. Inability to communicate with parents
2. Differences in attitudes (values generally, music, dress, solutions to problems, right and wrong)
3. Dating: whom, how many times a week, where, "I like him, but my parents don't")
4. Overprotection: parental unwillingness to sever the apron strings, inability to trust teener's judgment.
5. (Ties): Lack of respect for child's feelings
    Dictating relationships to others in the family.
    Lack of respect for teen preferences in dress and grooming.
6. Curfew!
7. (Tie): Use of car
    Friends we choose.

Parents listed these items as the main *points of tension* between themselves and their teen-age children:

1. Household responsibilities
2. Differences in values and attitudes
3. Lack of effective communication
4. Appearance (clothes, hair, makeup)
5. Freedom and restraint: a resentment of rules, and an inordinate desire for independence)
6. Intra-family tensions: Lack of respect, thoughtlessness.
7. "Others my age are doing it."
8. (Tie):
    Academic homework.
    Use of car and telephone.

Teen-agers listed as *the most effective disciplinary techniques* used by their parents as these:

1. Clear, consistent instructions, followed by parents' trusting the teener to follow those instructions.
2. Leading the child to accept responsibility for tasks in general and for conduct in particular.
3. Grounding!
4. Parental concern for teen-ager: "Where I am, with whom, what time to come in at night, pride in my good behavior, disappointment in my misbehavior."
5. Parental teaching of self-discipline and self-reliance.
6. Good example on the part of parents, inspiring their children to want to please parents and to admire them.

Parents, from their point of view, listed some of the same disciplinary techniques as being, in their judgment, most effective in rearing children:

1. Grounding (temporary withdrawal of privileges)
2. Corporal punishment through ages 10 or 11
3. (Tie):
   Giving clearest guidelines: what is expected, reward, penalty, reasons.
   Full explanation of wrong done when there is disobedience, trying to show causes and future results if wrong pattern continues.
4. Good parental example.
5. Relating freedom and responsibility: freedom when child acts responsibly, freedom withdrawn temporarily when child acts irresponsibly.
6. Continuing efforts to inculcate self-discipline.
7. Other factors: patience, understanding, humor in times of tenseness, prayer, faith.

Teen-agers, answering the question, "What could your parents do to help you to face your personal problems that they are not now doing?" gave these interesting suggestions:

1. Hear us through in a discussion of our problems and respect our point of view . . . that is, do not scorn it, ridicule it, or dismiss it without consideration.

2. *The second largest number of replies indicated that rapport with parents is so excellent that there is nothing more parents can do!*
3. Communicate with children more fully and clearly concerning *reasons why*. Perhaps, regular times of family discussions.
4. Just *listen* sometime without saying anything!
5. (Tie):

> Have respect for a teen-ager's need for privacy in living quarters, possessions, thoughts, plans.
>
> Greater sense of fair play in discussions and decisions: don't force teen-agers into an embarrassing situation from which there is no face-saving escape.

In the summary of the remainder of the questionnaire survey, there are many other interesting insights to the teen-agers' thoughts about themselves, their schools, their churches, the problems of young life, and some things they think can be done by church and school to assist teen-agers. (See pp. 134ff.)

2

Parents and Youth in Crisis

A group of us, invited to participate in a TV panel on youth problems, waited for the director of the panel, who had been delayed in a freeway traffic jam. Just at the "on the air" signal time, the breathless director of the panel arrived, rushed us into the studio; and, while thumbing furiously through her notebook to find her guidelines, she threw out this question to me: "Dr. Swor, what do you consider to be the largest single problem confronting young people of our day?"

Although I had often considered and discussed a list of youth problems, I had not pinpointed any one of the problems as the chief one. Suddenly, with a flash of inspiration of the sort which parents have had often when their children have asked questions for which, initially, parents thought they did not know the answer, this inspiration came: *Practically all the questionable activities of today's youth either arise through pressures from their peers or are facilitated by that pressure.* Therefore, I replied: "I feel that the greatest single problem of today's youth is pressure from those in their age group."

Several surveys have confirmed that the pressure to be accepted, to be popular, to be in the "in group" has been a tremendous factor in youth behavior. One survey included over 50,000 high school students. The makers of the survey concluded that the pressure of their peers is so heavy upon high school students that many of them will violate the teachings of their families and their churches and even the laws of society in preference to being called "chicken" or "clod" by their crowd.

Although to adults the fear of disapproval or rejection because of their convictions may seem an insufficient reason for succumbing to peer pressure, the fear is much greater and more determining to an adolescent. One writer has pointed out that fact in this way:

In some ways, temptation is more difficult for your child than for you. . . . This is particularly true in adolescence when "going along with the crowd" may reflect the child's need to be a part of the group. This group "is uncompromising in its demands that the adolescent conform to its standards of behavior and belief. It offers him in return a security or group belongingness!" If the Christian young person is in a distinct minority in his group, he has a tough battle to fight.[1]

The pressure of their peers is often only one of the pressures bearing upon young people. Some adult pressures on young people are: pressures from some parents for academic achievements as "bragging material"; pressures upon children to enter popularity contests, beauty contests, personality competition (the mamas have brought this sort of competition down to third and fourth graders these days!): pressures from some parents upon children to enter vocations of parent choosing.

To these pressures are added those of school activities, outside activities, and frequently dating pressures. Small wonder that so many of today's young people are like the title of a popular song of years ago, "Bewitched, Bothered, and Bewildered"! It is evident that young people who want to maintain a good balance between and among the many pressures of today must have some intelligent, helpful assistance from their parents.

Parents in Crisis, Too

But parents find themselves facing a harder-than-ever problem in seeking to guide their children; for, in addition to the strong peer pressure upon their children, parents find so often these additional difficulties:

1. *The deterioration of the time-honored respect in society for principles of honesty, sobriety, and sex morality.* The eyes and ears of their youngsters are bombarded constantly with episodes of well-known people who throw those principles to the wind, but who are apparently neither reproved nor penalized by society.

One young person said to me: "If adult America really believes that these things are wrong (the violations mentioned above), why do they not cry out against the people who do them? If it's acceptable for those prominent adults to commit these wrongs without penalty, why shouldn't young people have the same right?"

2. *The failure of other parents to hold firmly to right principles of character for their children, fearing a loss of favor with their children, and, therefore, becoming permissive toward principles so basic to strong character.* This laxness of some parents often leads children of wiser parents to feel that they are unduly restricted by their "old-fashioned parents." In many instances, permissive parents become vocally critical of the parents who insist upon the highest principles of character for their children, and this increases the problem of the wiser parents—particularly when "restricted" children point out that the indulgent parents are active church members, occasionally prominent in church leadership!

3. *The constant flow of wrong information and counsel in what young people hear, read, and see in movies, stage plays, and in everyday life.* The popular "situation ethics" emphasis seeks to lead young people to believe that the circumstances or situations and *not* absolute principles should determine decisions of right or wrong. Therefore, some young people question the absolute principles of their parents—principles derived largely from God's Word.

The "*Playboy* philosophy" regarding sex has had a distressingly large number of "takers" among young people. Increasingly, I receive this question in direct conversations with youth or through the question boxes: "It's not just marriage that gives one the right to sexual intercourse, is it? I thought that if two people just love each other, even if they're not married, they can have that privilege." Movies, magazines, and many best-seller books must share the responsibility for the promotion of this tragic philosophy; and many once character-strong colleges and universities are blameworthy for permitting, if not actually encouraging, sexual looseness through abandoning all dormitory restrictions and for tolerating some professors who boldly advocate the "free love" philosophy.

Against such sinister influences from so-called respectable sources—often presented cleverly and attractively—the concerned parent is called upon to stand firmly for honesty, sobriety, and sex morality.

Are There Any Allies?

Traditionally, the home, the school, and the church have been allies in the proclamation of the highest standards of conduct; and until comparatively recent years, those three institutions have stood firm in unity. What good parents taught in the home would be echoed in school and church: The youngster had no "escape" from the good counsel to right living!

Now, however, our public schools have suffered two crippling blows:

1. Public opinion has changed to the degree that a vocal group —not normally a majority of adults—can so criticize a school's actions or philosophies and can so threaten the school with court suits that many schools have felt obliged to drop, generally with great reluctance, some character-building emphases and activities, lest they be dragged through court trials for years.

2. Court actions and misinterpretations of those actions have forced schools to abandon some elements of both curriculum and student activity which formerly yielded distinct character strength to students.

Some of the finest men and women in America are in our public schools as administrators, counselors, and teachers; and many of them have said to me: "When we try to give even the basic guidelines to character, we are often criticized in letters from parents and at times even threatened by groups in the community." Regretfully, therefore, the public school cannot be as strong an ally to the home in character building as it once was—and as many of its leaders would like it to be now.

The church? Although the church has tried valiantly in many instances to offer strength to young people as an ally of the home in character building, it has suffered somewhat from these factors:

1. The proliferation of extra-curricular activities of schools and the mounting social activities have attracted young people at hours in which the church has planned activities for them.

2. The failure of the home often to cooperate with the church by emphasizing to their youngsters the importance of the youth-oriented activities of the church, urging their children to give some priority to the church-planned functions, has weakened the effectiveness of church appeals.

3. Another factor is the growing gap between the traditional strong character emphases of the church and the permissive emphasis of teen-age society, resulting in youth attitudes which range from mere discomfort in church meetings to open hostility toward the church. This problem has been complicated by the lagging alertness of many churches to communicate effectively to young people the wisdom and happiness involved in living by the highest principles. Without compromising principles, the church can communicate in more contemporary techniques, with the result that many young people actually would become enthusiastic about matters which now seem to bore them.

4. Although great numbers of churches are trying to make progress in bringing their preaching, teaching, and outreach to a finer relevance to today's needs, communicating more meaningfully to youth, young people who have loved the church and who continued in it have had in the past some justification for their complaint on the score of relevance. They have wanted the church

to reach out beyond its walls and traditional "intra-mural" functions to apply the compassion of Christianity to more daily needs and problems. Fortunately, many churches are responding to this challenge, and great numbers of young people are tackling school and community problems with enthusiasm and success under the guidance of their churches.

New Allies

New allies are appearing on the horizon to give hope and strength to the parents who want to uphold the principles of decent living for their children.

The most impressive new ally is the organized effort of many youth groups to insist upon decency in entertainment and publications slanted to youth. In massive rallies, over TV and radio, and through news media they have appealed to the "powers that be" to clean up dirty programs and publications.

In encouraging youth to abstain from tobacco and drugs some youth organizations have achieved notable success. In a California city, for instance, high school students leveled an attack upon cigarette smoking which captured the attention of a whole area and achieved notable results. In another California community, a high school girl arranged to permeate the community with a highly informative program on drug abuse. With the cooperation of school, newspapers, radio, and television, she and other young people gave every young person in the area sufficient information to remove any possible excuse for drug abuse.

Other allies to parents who are striving to "hold the line" in maintaining wise standards of character and conduct for their children are these:

1. Some psychiatrists and psychologists who deal with teen-age problems are pointing out that youngsters who are reared by strict but wise parents are much better adjusted, happier, and more given to leadership qualities at the junior and senior high school level than teen-agers of permissive parents.

2. Junior and senior high school counselors from throughout America have told me that they can "spot" quickly individuals in the two groups: those students wisely reared and those reared indulgently.

3. Some widely-read and respected columnists, cartoonists, and other journalists who command the reading public's eye and ear are adding the impact of their appeal to the plea to maintain or restore wise parental authority.

4. In many communities, parents' leagues or groups are being formed with the purpose of agreeing upon standards for young people of the junior and senior high ages, thereby giving guidelines for the conduct of students and protection for the parents against the "but other young people are doing it" complaint.

Although these allies to parents are most timely and welcome, the home will always be the area in which, first of all and most of all, convictions need to be instilled, courage needs to be developed, and motivation for right living needs to be imparted. Therefore, it is in the all-important world of home that the major work for building strong character must occur.

Cultivating Decision Strength

The strength to say no to the many pressures upon young people to unwise or dangerous action cannot be "imparted" by the parent as if it were a birthday gift. That strength has to be cultivated in a continuing process of teaching through good two-way communication. In this continuing communication, the parents need to be "sure of their ground" in the matter of why certain principles are right and why certain practices are wrong, infinitely patient in discussing and repeating and reemphasizing, and willing to hear their children state their positions and reasons with respect.

Robert H. Lauer in an article, "Teach Your Child to Say No," suggests that the discussions concerning the child's involvement in activities about which there are questions may revolve around these questions: [2]

1. *What kind of person do you want to be? What is your ideal of manhood or womanhood?*

Mr. Lauer quotes William James, distinguished American psychologist and educator: "Sow an action and you reap a habit; sow a habit and you reap a character; sow a character and you reap a destiny." If the youngster can be helped to see that any actions involving principle will help significantly to make him either strong or weak in adulthood, this long look may be a constraining factor. Pointing out adults whom he admires, and sharing any knowledge at hand concerning the growing up years of such adults can be a most tangible teaching element.

2. *What kind of relationship do you want to have with others?*

In this regard, writer Lauer says: "The question refers both to the peer group and to the date. . . . Does he want to flow in easily with the group and avoid the difficulty of making his own decisions? Does he want to be nothing more than a droplet in a swiftly moving stream? Or does he want to be himself? Does he want to retain his individuality?"

Mr. Lauer points out that since young people prize highly the right to make their own decisions in relationship to parental teaching, parents may well seek to show the teen-ager that he should place the same high value upon making independent decisions in relationships to his peers and to his dates, assuring the teener that this course of action will ultimately bring genuine respect from those who matter most to him.

3. *Is it worth it?* Lauer sees this as crucial:

Sometimes young people think only in terms of immediate satisfaction, and neglect to look a little further into the consequences. . . . In terms of consequence, is it worth it? Will the action help or hinder the development of one's personality into what he wants to be? . . . Is it worth it to sacrifice inner strength on the altar of group approval?

In such matters as smoking, liquor, drugs, gambling, speed

driving, physical promiscuity on dates, cheating, and other temptations which come to almost all teen-agers in our day, parents can gather a sheaf of true-to-life reports of consequences from newspapers, magazines, local court records, surveys, studies, and occasional TV presentations. Although the news of marriages of teen-agers because of pregnancies will not appear in the local press, the news is generally quite well known and can be shared with recalcitrant teeners as an illustration of consequences.

4. *Why do you want to do this?*

Do you feel insecure with the group and feel that you must do this as a kind of "crutch" to boost your ego, to make yourself feel more comfortable with the group, to seek through compromise of principle which you know to be right to advance your standing with the group? Do you want to do it just because of hostility toward your parents?

If This Isn't Enough?

In pointing out that many young people will be persuaded by discussions revolving around those four questions, Mr. Lauer raises a relevant question concerning the youngster who doesn't accept the findings connected with those discussions: "But what if he doesn't?" He answers the question thus: "There are times, therefore, when you will have to exercise your veto and make your child's decisions for him. . . . But this veto power must be used sparingly, for only as your child has the strength and insight to make his own healthy decisions will he be able to live soberly, righteously, and godly in this world."

Mr. Lauer concludes his discussion with the reminder that parents can help their youngsters to see that their choices involving the crowd offer these possibilities: (1) to comply with the standards and wishes of the crowd, (2) to stand alone in the face of pressure, and (3) to choose a new group that has different standards. Group acceptance and participation are of great significance to growing youngsters; therefore, parents will want to do their best to help their teen-agers make the decisions which will give them needful group involvement but without compromise of important principles.

Lastly, encourage your teen-ager to read the chapter, "How to Say No," in Evelyn Millis Duvall's book, *Facts of Life and Love for Teen-agers,* listed in Chapter 10.

3

Home: The Soil and Climate

Good soil and favorable climate plus intelligent tilling will, with the fewest exceptions, produce good grain and fruit. An occasional bad plant or instance of underdeveloped fruit may occur, but these instances are almost negligible in comparison with the abundance of good, wholesome products.

The soil and climate in which parents will cultivate children, the fruit of marriage, are *the character and atmosphere of the home.* Although the impact of the makeup of the home may have been expressed in more technical, sociological, and psychological terms, it has never been expressed more meaningfully than in this statement which has appeared widely in bulletins, magazines, and newspapers:

If a child lives with criticism, he learns to condemn;
If a child lives with hostility, he learns to fight;
If a child lives with ridicule, he learns to be shy;
If a child lives with shame, he learns to feel guilty;
If a child lives with tolerance, he learns to be patient;
If a child lives with encouragement, he learns confidence;
If a child lives with praise, he learns to appreciate;
If a child lives with fairness, he learns justice;
If a child lives with security, he learns to have faith;
If a child lives with approval, he learns to like himself;
If a child lives with acceptance and friendship, he learns to find love in the world.

Dr. Charles Wahl, an eminent professor of psychiatry, is reported by Associated Press to have made this significant declaration in a Los Angeles address: "Personal maturity and the capacity to love and work are primarily developed, not through sociologic factors directly, but through a loving and secure relationship within the biological family."

Continuing the emphasis upon the impact which the character and atmosphere of the home make upon the children, a group of psychiatrists in a Midwestern city, upon studying a group of disturbed teen-agers in relation to home atmosphere, made this observation:

> Good communication within the family seemed to be a major factor in helping the teen-ager adjust to his problems and in meeting the goals his parents had set for him. Conversely, it was poor communication that seemed to increase the anxieties of disturbed adolescents. Carried to extremes, these breakdowns in family communications could result in the need for psychiatric help.[1]

In my years as a counselor on a college campus, I never encountered a serious problem with students who had come from homes in which excellent rapport between parents and children had existed and in which the youngsters growing up had felt secure, were well disciplined and adequately instructed, were aware of being genuinely loved, and who admired their parents greatly. The soil and climate of such homes had produced well-adjusted young people who, in the many opportunities for weakness during college years, never really lost their way.

Two parents whose son was being tried for a series of dastardly crimes said to a reporter: "We can't understand why he did these things. We always gave him everything he wanted." It is entirely possible that they did just that, but that they did not give him everything he *needed* in character development. The home which does not have genuine character strength is a poor prospect for producing children of strength and joy.

Since the two people who will determine the quality of homelife are the parents, let's examine the role of parents in providing the soil and climate so needful for growing well-adjusted children.

Parents as Persons

Do you remember the clever observation, "Character is both taught and caught"? And I would like to add this observation: Little of character teaching will be effective if the children in a family do not "catch" the character spirit from good examples of their parents. In my survey of teen-agers, I found that they put tremendous emphasis upon the example impact of parents in effectiveness of character teaching, in discipline, and in the total of influences which guided their lives.

A young seminary student who was spending the summer in his hometown was asked to minister to a nearby rural church which had been polarized into two hostile groups. As he called upon members of the little church, he identified himself as the son of a Christian businessman with whom almost all of them had had business dealings and whom they admired greatly for his Christian character. Regardless of which "side" of the breach in the church a person happened to claim, he or she received the young man happily because of admiration for his father.

In sharing the foregoing episode with me the young minister said: "If they had had opportunity to know my mother, they would have had the same high regard for her. My parents loved God, they loved each other, they loved their children, they taught us well; but, best of all, they *lived* what they taught so winsomely, that everything they asked of us we knew to be right." *There is no substitute for good example!*

The National Fathers Committee offered an excellent "Ten Commandments for Fathers" in a recent year. Here is the suggestion:

By my example—
1. I shall teach my child respect for his fellowman.
2. I shall teach him good sportsmanship in work and play.

3. I shall instill in him an appreciation of religion and the family as the backbone of society.
4. I shall strive for companionship and mutual understanding.
5. I shall impart to him a desire to love and honor his country and to obey its laws.
6. I shall encourage him to apply himself to difficult jobs.
7. I shall teach him the importance of participation in community affairs and local government.
8. I shall teach him self-reliance and help him develop an independent spirit.
9. I shall help him develop a sense of responsibility in planning for the future.
10. I shall, above all, teach him the duties and responsibilities of citizenship in a free society.

By my example!

Pinpointing additionally the impact of a parent's character upon youngsters through good parental example, Mr. Dennis Hoover, news staff writer for the *Dallas Morning News,* said in an article, "Parents Set Road Example":

What can you, a parent, do to immunize your teen-ager against accidents? More than anybody else, say the experts.

First, you can set a good example. Your attitudes about safety, respect for the law and other people begin to rub off on your children when they're quite young.

If you cheat at stop signs, whip the car around like you're always in a hurry, act rudely toward other drivers, receive traffic tickets and cuss policemen, it must be all right (the youngsters will probably think).

"Even such a seemingly minor thing as a parent parking in a no parking zone helps in developing attitudes in the observant young. . . ."

"By the time a boy becomes a teen-ager it's late to tell him how he ought to drive. He's been watching you since he was two years old," said Judge Carl Friedlander, who presides over Dallas' Teen-age Traffic Court.[2]

If the parent as a *person* is strong, consistent, winsome, loving, and lovable in *character,* his or her example will be the greatest single factor in validating parental teaching, discipline, and companionship.

Two boys, brothers, asked me on a college campus if I knew their dad. At the time, I did not know him. In evident regret that I had missed knowing the great man in their lives, they said to me: "We wish you knew our dad. He is the most wonderful person we've ever known. We'd rather go hunting, fishing, golfing with dad than with anybody else." While my heart sang a paean of thanks for a parent who, among other things, is a companion to his children, they continued: "You just couldn't grow up around our dad without *wanting* to do right."

"Wanting to do right" because of the contagious character quality of a parent's example: that is the compliment supreme which every parent should strive to merit!

Parents as Partners

Another source of strength which parents can give to their children is the living example of a happy marriage. Their strength and attractiveness as individual personalities and their congeniality and effectiveness *as a team* can give security to developing youngsters, can relieve them of anxieties concerning the future, and can give to them better intelligence and strength for planning their own marriages than a college major in sociology *without* the privilege of having grown up around parents who were *partners* in the fullest and happiest sense of the word.

Parents need to be partners in the ideals for character, which having lived, they teach to their children. They need to be partners in establishing codes of conduct, and they need to be in accord in disciplinary matters. They need to maintain mutual respect in the presence of their children, ironing out their personal disagreements in privacy. They need to demonstrate toward each other courtesy, thoughtfulness, patience, love, and forgiveness, for what they are to each other in personal relationships will automatically become their children's concept of marriage.

Also as partners, parents need some reasonable interests and activities outside the home, adding a dimension of interest to their

lives and to the interest of their children in their parents' achievements. Some of these outside interests can well be interests which
involve the parents together while other interests can involve
them separately in activities which appeal uniquely to men or
to women. Just as it is tragic for parents to be so much involved
in outside interests that their children feel themselves to be sec-
ondary in importance to their parents, it can become most unfortunate for either or both of the parents to become so completely "wrapped up" in the children that they cease to grow
together as a parent team.

UPI reports an address by Dr. Alfred A. Messer, of Emory
University, in which parents were urged to balance wholesome
concern and adequate involvement with their children with sufficient outside activities as adults. He pointed out that if parents
have lived only in a children's world for twenty years, not growing in mutual interests which tie them together as adults, the
departure of the children from home may well find two adult
strangers living together with no mutual interests and activities
which have grown through the years. The UPI article concluded:
"He called for more adult times—more second honeymoons and
more activities for parents in their role as spouses rather than in
their role as parents."

The reporter had these clever words in the last paragraph: "You
heard what the doctor said. Have some fun. Some honest to goodness adult fun—without the children."

"Parents as partners" can well review these "Ten Rules for a
Happy Marriage," found in various publications.

1. Be stingy with your criticism, but lavish with your praise, one unto
   the other.
2. Never criticize your mate in public.
3. Keep petty troubles to yourself, for they are family affairs and often
   not even worth worrying about yourself.
4. Put your mate's happiness before your own.
5. Plan things together, for you are a team now.

6. Never make major decisions without talking the matter over together, because marriage is a partnership.
7. Plan little surprises for each other. Actions like these say without words, "I Love You."
8. Take an interest in civic affairs.
9. Take God into your marriage. Work together, play together, pray together, so as to have a marriage that stays together.
10. Be considerate of your in-laws. Remember, you are an in-law yourself.

Children who grow up in a home in which their parents are partners in the fullest, happiest sense will have a wonderful advantage in the important matter of security.

The Parent as a Parent

In the early years of a child's experiences parents can and should be the overwhelming influence in the child's concepts of life, in his codes of conduct, in his relationships to others, and in his anticipation of the future. Although, as pointed out earlier, far more "outside" influences impinge upon children now than ever before, it is still possible for parents to be the determining formulators of guidelines for their children. And, beyond the child's childhood years, wise parents can continue to be the greatest stabilizing force in the lives of their offspring.

Although many books have been written and more will be written concerning parent-child relationships from the viewpoint of parental responsibilities, here is a partial list of obligations involved in parenthood:

1. To develop a dynamic, growing knowledge from which to draw in dealing with children.

This knowledge will include the knowledge of ideals for character and conduct; a knowledge validated in the parents' personal living experiences; a knowledge of characteristics of age periods in a child's life with variations understood to be normal when there are two or more children in the family; a knowledge of the chief needs for instruction, discipline, and affection of children at various stages of their growth; a thorough knowledge of the contemporary pressures, temptations, and challenges which children of our day must face.

In addition to indispensable common sense, parents can obtain knowledge in these areas from the Bible, from books (see resource book lists at conclusion of this book), from magazine and newspaper articles, from parent seminars, from conversations with other successful parents, and from good rapport with their own children. The knowledge which helps men and women become good parents is, of course, not static, but, rather, dynamic and growing as they keep contact with the sources of knowledge mentioned above.

In a symposium on "How The Bible Can Help Us Solve Today's Problems" Dr. Norman Vincent Peale recommended a strong "dose" of biblical instruction to strengthen us against the deterioration about us: "The most pressing problem confronting our country today is the deterioration of character among our people—young and old. Our problems stem basically from moral laxity. We need to restore the old-fashioned emphasis on character in the making of a strong people and a strong nation."[3]

For ideals for living, for reminders to parents concerning the importance of instruction and discipline, and for counsel to young people concerning their relationships to God and man, the Bible has no peer. If parents are living those ideals, if they are communicating them to their children, if they are relating biblical ideals in a highly relevant manner to today's problems, they can be sure that they have imparted to their children the best of knowledge for character and conduct.

A knowledge of age characteristics, personality differences, needs of successive age levels, problems of special kinds—handicaps, retardation, the gifted child, the slow learner, the late bloomer, and unseen defects, for instance—and the particular difficulties of adolescence can be achieved through reading and from consultation with others. I have prepared a rather extensive reading and resource list in the last chapter of this book. But, even before this book is off the press, there will be other publications of relevance; therefore, the growing knowledge, which the parent desires will prompt the parent to keep an open, eager eye for continuing publications.

2. *To impart instruction.*

Since the learning process for a child begins in infancy and continues, hopefully, through the years and since parents are the child's first and, let us hope, best teachers, the role of the parent in imparting guidance for life and its problems is a vastly important one. Later chapters will discuss instruction in some of today's most pressing youth needs.

3. *To attend to discipline.*

In view of the probability that a youngster's respect for law and the rights of others will be a reflection of the respect which he learned (or didn't learn) in respecting the rules, persons, and property in his homelife, wise discipline is a major responsibility of parents. A later chapter will discuss this responsibility in detail.

4. *To develop courage.*

In contemporary life parents need a very real courage to stand by convictions for child-rearing which are imperative to rearing children with strong character principles. So many other parents will not stand firmly by those same principles, and this creates the situation in which the children of the courageous ones may pressure their parents to "be like Johnny's parents."

Surely, you have read somewhere the tongue-in-cheek and inspiringly delightful article, "World's Meanest Mother." In a rollicking sense of mock criticism, but of infinite implied admiration for that mother, the writer of the piece pointed out that her mother had the courage to rear her children by the wisest ideals, despite what the other children's parents permitted them to do:

My mother insisted on knowing where we were at all times. . . . She insisted that if we said we'd be gone for an hour, that we would be gone one hour or less. . . . She made us work! We had to wash dishes, make beds, learn to cook and all sorts of cruel things. . . . She always insisted on our telling the truth, the whole truth, and nothing but the truth. . . . None of the tooting of the horn of a car for us to come running. She embarrassed us by making our dates and friends come to the door to get us. . . . While my friends were dating at the mature age of 12 or 13, my old-fashioned mother refused to let me date until I was 15 or 16. . . .

My mother was a complete failure as a mother. None of us has ever been arrested. . . . Each of my brothers served his time in the service of his country. . . . Look at the things we missed. We never got to take part in a riot, burn draft cards and a million and one things that our friends did. . . . She made us grow up into God-fearing, educated, honest adults.

The anonymous woman writer who composed this delightful essay concluded it with these challenging words: Using this as a background, I am trying to raise my children. I stand a little taller and I am filled with pride when my children call me mean. You see, I thank God that He gave me the meanest mother in the world.

The *Phoenix* (Arizona) *Gazette,* which carried the foregoing article, added this editorial comment: "From this, I would say the country doesn't need a 5-cent cigar: it needs more 'mean' mothers . . . and dads."[4]

5. *To provide time for two important opportunities to meet needs which are not met in some families:*

a. Time to listen unhurriedly, eagerly, understandingly to the individual child's desire to share or discuss or ask something which to the child at that time is probably more important than a busy parent realizes. In my survey of teen-agers' relationships to their parents, the need and hunger to be "listened to" were expressed frequently, as in these replies:

They could have discussed the facts of life with me when I was small, but they didn't; so, now I do not feel free to talk with them.

One of the main problems is their 'passing off' certain teen-age problems as being merely 'a part of growing up.' This is a serious mistake on the part of parents.

Talk to us. Ask questions. Get to know what we want, not what they think we want.

We could set aside a time every week just to discuss things that anybody in the family would want to discuss.

I don't feel that my parents take my problems seriously; so, if my problem isn't too big, I keep it to myself or discuss it with friends.

My parents would rather play cards than to see me in a play.

And how refreshing are these different voices:

They're great, because we can talk to each other.

I feel that my parents are doing all that is possible now in helping me to face my problems. *They are always ready to listen.*

They help me so much. I share with them, and we pray together. They are there whenever I need them.

There is nothing more my parents can do for me now. My parents have already prepared me in earlier years; therefore, the temptations which 'floor' most young people do not surprise or bother me.

My parents are fantastic, and I don't think they could do much more.

This may sound idealistic, but my parents are doing all they can to listen to me and to help me face my problems.

b. Time to plan for activities involving the whole family. In the frenziedly busy days in which we live, planning family-centered activities requires ingenuity, persuasiveness, and even "pulling one's rank"; but parents who do not plan times of family fellowship, fun, and activity rob themselves and their children of one of the best chances for building family unity, for getting to know each other in an atmosphere of relaxed enjoyment, and for providing materials of which some of the happiest memories are made.

One of our nation's busiest professional men and his much-sought-after wife (book reviews, church activities, and clubs) declared Thursday evenings to be "family evening" for their family. No member of the family ever accepted an invitation to any outside activity for that evening. Busy mother and dad said smilingly, but firmly, "We have an important appointment with our children that evening, and we wouldn't think of breaking it." The children, sensing something of the city-wide significance of their parents, felt happy and honored that *they* were preferred to everybody else that night!

What did they do on Thursday evenings? If they had voted to stay at home, the children decided the dinner menu and the entertainment they would enjoy. If the family voted to go out for the evening, various members of the family circle expressed preferences; and, sooner or later, the family got around to everybody's preference. The children were allowed the major voice in these determinations; therefore, even when some of them were in senior high, they preferred Thursday evenings with their family to other activities. One by one, each of the children invited a Thursday evening guest, sharing the family-centered joy.

Summer weeks provide a variation, because the children are available in afternoons or for an occasional all-day jaunt. If you would like a wealth of ideas for planning family activities, you will find a number of suggestions in the resource book list at the conclusion of this book, listed under the heading "Family Centered Activities."

6. *To bestow affection and to provide companionship.*

As pointed out in several parts of this volume, parents should strive to let a very real sense of love go through all of their relationships as a golden cord—even in times of disagreement, reproof, and chastisement. The poorest parent in the world who gives evidence of a stable, unwavering love is giving to the child a much more valuable gift than the richest parent who seeks to lavish material gifts upon a child in lieu of love.

A young adult, now married and looking forward to a family of his own, said to me: "When my parents took what I as a teenager thought of as too much care about what I did, where I went, and with whom I went, and who occasionally withdrew privileges and administered punishment, they always made very clear to me that they were doing what they were doing because they loved me more than they loved their own lives, and that they so much wanted me to grow up to be a strong man. Although, as a teen-ager, I thought that they overdid the caring, explaining, and punishing, of one thing I was always sure: *they loved me very much,* and I would never have been tempted to join the "love and flower people" to find love. I experienced it day by day in all relationships with my wonderful parents. If I can be just like them to my children, I shall consider myself a most successful parent."

In suggesting that parents give companionship to their children I mean the spending of some time with the children *on their terms,* doing things which the children enjoy. The busy man who spends some time after work hours in pitching baseballs to his eager son, or in matching skills in tossing the basketball through the hoop on the garage gable, or in making model planes, or in hunting or fishing or golfing is giving a quality of companionship which makes home a special place for the son.

The equally busy mother who pitches in to help her daughter in girl-type hobbies, putting herself enthusiastically and companionably into the activity, has created an atmosphere in which good rapport will develop and in which good character training will occur.

Companionship does *not* mean that the parents are trying to be big sister or big brother, for that relationship is not the role of the parent. Children need pals of their own ages, and the parent who mistakenly tries to take the place of those same-age pals is creating a false relationship. Children can get plenty of pals of their age; from parents they want and seek an entirely different level of companionship—one which gives them strength, guidance, and assurance.

Speaking of the "faked relationship" existing when parents try to act like teen-agers or to barge into the teen-age friendships of their youngsters, NEA quoted an unnamed psychiatrist thus:

It's important for parents to try to understand their teen-agers, but wrong for parents to try to be a part of the teen-ager world. . . . If the parents will just accept their role, they will have a lot more influence with their children than if they try to pretend there isn't any difference. . . . And how can parents expect teen-agers to look forward to being adults if the parents seem to think so little of maturity that they try to act like teen-agers themselves?[5]

To summarize: adult companions, *yes*. . . . Teen-age pals, *no!*

7. *To maintain a vital personal interest in the interests, aspirations, concerns, and problems of each child in the family.*

This vital personal interest can be more of an attitude and a disposition than a great deal of parental initiative in opening conversations with individual children about their thoughts. Being accessible when the child wants to talk, giving evidence in the conversation that you have done thinking about his or her concern since the last conversation, finding information from other sources to place at the child's disposal, making possible his having contact with individuals—groups—activities which will facilitate his development—but, above all, helping the child to know that what he is thinking and planning really *matters* to you. These are the traits which indicate meaningful parental interest.

"But," some reader exclaims, "where in the world will a parent find the time to do all these things, what with all the chores and plain everyday bread-winning we have to do?"

My frank reply is this: You did not have the right to bring your children into this world of pressure and confusion without accepting the responsibility to help them in every way possible to grow up into maximum strength. It may take personal sacrifice to make the time available; but, since parents have their children few enough years, they must meet their need for maximum constructive attention now, saving the years when the children have gone from home to indulge themselves in activities and interests which are currently responsible for denying children full parental involvement in their interests. *While it is essential that parents have some interests outside the home and without the children, and such activities can be arranged by wise parents, it is of transcending importance that parents find the time or make the time to maintain this indispensable personal interest in the interests of each child in the family.*

8. *To know when to "let go."*

The time must come inevitably for parents, having done their best for their children, to trust them to live their own lives and make their own choices and decisions, trusting them to weave into their maturing lives the example, teaching, and concern which their parents have invested in them. Although this may well be one of the greatest emotional struggles parents encounter, the letting-go is essential to the full maturing process. If there are several children in a family, the letting-go age may vary with individuals, since individuals may mature at different speeds; but when the time comes, parents will be doing the child a favor to "send him on his way" with confidence and love.

Parents as Teachers

Long before the child learns to read and write and long before he enters school, some of life's most important lessons need to be taught, and needs which will come into focus in the teen and later years can be approached through parental instruction. For particular focus in this volume, however, we shall confine our discussion of the instruction needs of children in the matters of *honesty, sex, liquor, drugs, tobacco.* To these considerations the next three chapters will be given.

4

Parents Teaching . . .

Honesty: "As the Crow Flies"

In the early evening in one of our cities, the T.V. programs of local stations were interrupted with an emergency bulletin. Someone had seen an adult scooping up two children, putting them in the trunk of the car, and speeding rapidly away westward. "Check immediately to see if your children are at home. . . . Look out, everybody, for a car of this description. . . . Advise law enforcement officers of any information which will lead to the apparent kidnappers," said the announcers with evident excitement.

A whole city went on search—parents for any children not at home, neighbors for their neighbors' children, citizens in western areas looking for the car described by the announcer. Many parents wept at the thought of two precious children put rudely into a dark and stuffy car trunk, terrified of possible disaster. Switchboards of police headquarters and of radio and TV stations were jammed with calls. Many parents whose children were safe prayed fervently in a sense of vicarious suffering for the parents of the apparently kidnapped children.

Relief, chagrin, and some serious thoughts concerning the implications came in the 10 P.M. news announcement. The apparent kidnappers were parents, putting their own two children in the trunk of the car, so that they could drive in to a drive-in movie without paying for tickets for the two children! The car had been found in the drive-in movie with the entire family enjoying the entertainment, including the two children, now "untrunked," well, and happy!

The foregoing true episode is a vignette of the society in which our children are growing up today: rampant dishonesty, abetted by a throng of adults, leaving youngsters with the feeling that anything they can get by with is acceptable. Only "getting caught" is to be deplored. The line between honesty and dishonesty has never been as vague in the history of our nation; therefore, the challenge to parents who wish to rear children with a strong sense of integrity is tremendous.

The picture is dark, indeed. Such a wave of embezzlements as our nation has never experienced has occurred in recent years, involving in a majority of instances men and women who had been highly regarded by their firms and by the communities. Employee thefts in stores and other businesses have become a national scandal. Shoplifting by people who are otherwise respectable people has reached such proportions that many stores have been obliged to instal expensive thief-catching electronic equipment. Grocery stores in a large metropolitan area of our country announced in full-page ads in a recent holiday season that the stores were losing a half-million dollars regularly in thefts in comparatively brief periods. Some formerly highly respected professional men, some men high in government, and even some educators have been sent to prison for dishonesties.

The Child's School World

In recent years, I have visited high schools from Hawaii to Maryland; and, wherever I have gone, I have learned from counselors and principals that the problem of dishonesty in schools has become unbelievably large. The constant refrain is this: a higher percentage of students than ever before admit to at least occasional cheating (67% to 92% in some schools which made anonymous surveys); when apprehended, almost no students show regret for the dishonesty . . . they only regret being apprehended; dishonesties in abuse and theft of library materials, theft in cafeterias, theft of student property, slugs in vending machines, deception, and general destruction of property are frequent.

Beyond the school ground and school hours, so many school officials report, shoplifting groups (so often involving young people of excellent economic families), and other forms of dishonesty "just for kicks" are frequent. One of the saddest aspects of these widespread acts of dishonesty in both school and community is that the pressure of teen-agers upon each other frequently leads a teen-ager to participate in the dishonest practice "to be a good sport" or to keep from being called "chicken"!

Crisis? Indeed!

In view of the confusion wrought by advocates of situation ethics—"no absolutes," they say—in view of the conflicting advice which abounds in the young person's hearing, and in view of the frequent disappointment of young people in adults whom they have respected, it has become imperative for the home to establish and teach some unmistakable standards of honesty. The alternative to such teaching is to send youngsters out into life with no sound basis for honest living and with a susceptibility to being a statistic in the rolls of the dishonorable.

Project into the future the life of a child who has fuzzy ideas in the matter of honesty, or who does not have a deep conviction that honesty is a supreme virtue. He or she cannot be a good marriage partner, for these is no stable marriage without implicit trust, a trust which dishonesty makes impossible. Career is endangered, for dishonesty can make some dishonest practices seem right. Reputation is jeopardized, for the individual without a clear concept of honesty may fall afoul of society's laws any day. *The whole future of one's children is involved in the important responsibility of teaching honesty!*

What Is Honesty?

One of the age-old laws of teaching is this: "The teacher must know that which he would teach." The clearer the concept of honesty is in the mind and experience of the parent, the more clearly he can teach that concept to his children.

Some years ago, Dr. Richard C. Cabot authored a book with the one-word title, *Honesty,* in which some timeless truths concerning honesty were defined and discussed most helpfully. Here are some of Dr. Cabot's definitions:

Honesty: The will and the effort to keep one's agreements, explicit and tacit. It can be expressed in words (veracity), or in actions as fulfilment of contracts, and in habits such as fidelity, loyalty, and punctuality.

A Lie: An attempt to deceive without consent (of the person to whom one is talking or writing). It may not succeed; yet, if it tries to deceive, it is a lie from the moment that it crosses the liar's lips.

Prevarication: The attempt to convey a false impression to one's hearer by words which in some other sense are true.

Equivocation: The use of a word which has two meanings. The equivocator intends that the hearer shall grasp one meaning, while the other is true in the case in hand.

Evasion: In which one avoids saying anything on a subject that he does not wish to talk about. This can be done by changing the subject.

Internal Honesty: The effort to think straight, to record and to develop truly what one finds wandering in through the senses, what one has done, what has happened, what one has learned in conversation, in books, and in one's own thoughts.[1]

Quite naturally, the foregoing definitions cannot be shared in just those words with the younger children in a family; yet, parents can do two things with those definitions: (1) they can so thoroughly subscribe to the principles in their own lives that conveying them to the children will be but an overflow of their lives and not a "do as I say, not as I do" situation; (2) they can change the wording to language which children understand.

What Is Honesty's Scope?

An individual is not truly honest unless he is honest toward God, toward his inner best self, and toward his fellowman. Honesty toward God will lead the individual to take care of his God-given body, developing it fully, keeping it free from defiling and degrading factors; to develop his mental capacities (including talents) to the limit, to use them in God-honoring ways, to be intellectually honest, to keep the mind free from defilement; to develop spiritual capacities all through life, to appropriate God's wisdom through Bible study, to develop power through the privilege of prayer, to discern and follow God's will in all areas of one's life, to be a good steward of time—money—talent. These are some facets of honesty toward God.

Honesty toward one's inner best self will impel the individual to obey "the voice of God within him," called by various names —conscience, self-respect, inner best self. If the individual fails to heed or fails to obey that inner best self long enough, the signals will become fainter and will be silenced eventually, leading to a state of self-deceit.

Dr. Cabot pointed out in his excellent book that internal dishonesty "rots him (the individual)," and a splendid psychiatrist long ago pointed out that self-deceit is probably the most common sin of man—and a stupid sin, at that, observed the psychiatrist.

Honesty toward fellowman will lead the individual to want to *tell the truth* in word and action in *all* of his relationships to other people—individuals, groups, society, government. This aspect of honesty will be impossible, we see, if the individual has lost the battle for honesty within his own mind and heart. It is in the matter of honesty in daily communications and dealings that parents will have their first and, perhaps, best opportunities to teach the principles of honesty.

How Vast Is Honesty's Significance?

Dr. Cabot, mentioned earlier, feels that the significance of honesty is so great, that he epitomizes honesty and dishonesty thus: *Honesty* is "the king of virtues," indicating that honesty is the basic strength of life, from which all other strengths must develop. *Lying* is "the king of vices," indicating that the dishonest person is susceptible to all kinds of weaknesses in thinking and acting.

From a lifetime of distinguished service as the nation's top law enforcement official, J. Edgar Hoover in an article, "If I Had a Son," once expressed essentially this same conviction. Hoover said that if he had a son, he would "teach him not to lie to me; and, furthermore, I would not lie to him." With volumes of crime statistics to sustain his conviction of the vast significance of dishonesty in crime—particularly youth crime, Mr. Hoover equated honesty with respect for and obedience to law and the rights of others.

Or, to put the matter tersely: *Honesty,* ingrained in the character of children, will safeguard every fine teaching of parents, will "insure" the children against character breakdowns and attendant dishonor in the future, and will contribute to society pillars of strength to safeguard society's integrity. With no thought of reflecting upon the concluding verse of chapter 13 of 1 Corinthians, but with a desire to pinpoint the vast significance of honesty, I suggest: "Now we have before us materials, success, fame, and honesty . . . but the greatest of these is honesty!"

Teaching Honesty: How Soon?

As all of us know, children vary in perception and in memory capacity; therefore the ability to *understand* and to *remember* will determine the child's susceptibility to effective teaching.

Flora Rheta Schreiber, in an article titled "Memory: Clue to Your Child's Development," points out a factor which many parents either do not know or that they forget: "A child's behaviour is conditioned by the stage of memory development he has reached."[2] She points out splendidly the growing capacity to remember—from the first year, in which "memories are simply responses to direct appeals to the senses and to strong emotional experiences, chiefly painful ones, to the virtually adult memory he acquires in his fifth year." Also, she points out that the major gain of the fifth year is the ability to remember concepts.

Wise parents will sense the varying capacities of their children to understand and to remember, and will begin the important matter of teaching *why* a thing is honest or dishonest as early as the comprehension and memory capacity permit. Prior to the capacity to understand concepts, however, the parent will be quick to correct dishonesties, even if the child is not yet able to understand *why*. Therefore, we may say that the teaching should begin as early as the child can understand, and the expectation of obedience should begin as soon as the child can remember the concepts taught.

Teaching Honesty: How?

The reply to the question, *"How?"* is simple: by parental example and constant teaching of the principle of honesty. The example of parents in this regard is not only indispensable, but, also, the determinant of the seriousness with which children will believe and follow parental teaching. It is at this point that the cause of honesty suffers a tragic blow. Wide eyes, listening ears, and remembering minds observe dishonesty in speech, law observance, and everyday dealings with one's world on the part of parents; and, after so long a time, the youngsters inevitably assume that dishonesty is the accepted way of life.

On the other hand, observance of honesty in the parents' daily relationships throughout the growing-up years can condition the child's mind to the importance of honesty. My mother, widowed and poverty-stricken in an age in which there was no social security or aid to dependent children, was so scrupulously honest that, on a number of occasions, she walked back to town—a mile away—to take a few cents of excess change which a clerk had given. Once I brought home 17¢ too much change from one transaction; and, upon counting out the change, she said, "This is not our money, and we would be stealing to keep it." Having walked a mile to the stores and a mile back, now to be dispatched on another two-mile jaunt to return 17¢ made an impression unforgettable: *it matters to be honest.*

With parental example clear in the matter of honesty, parents are in position to teach the principles of honesty—abstractly at first, applied to specific instances later. The teachings of the Bible, the definitions of such writers as Dr. Cabot, and the wealth of adages, proverbs, and illustrative stories will provide a wealth of teaching material. From my earliest days I remember hearing at home, at church, and at school such statements as "Honesty is always the best policy," "It is better to fail honestly than to succeed dishonestly," "A lie will always catch up with you," and similar ones. Romans 12:17 and Romans 13:13 came into my mind through teachings in my childhood: "Provide things honest in the sight of all men," and "Let us walk honestly, as in the day."

Doubtless, the most impressive and best remembered teaching on honesty will come in the application of the abstract principles to experiences in a child's life. A distinguished university president had the parent-taught principle of honesty put into "concrete" form both figuratively and literally during his childhood. In returning to his residence one day, he picked up a piece of concrete from the yard of a residence up the street, assuming that the people who lived there had discarded it. When his parents discovered what he had done, they helped him to see that the concrete, picked up on a neighbor's yard, did not belong to him; and that, though he was evidently not conscious that he had done so, he had taken someone's property, and that is stealing. If that now-distinguished educator chances to read these lines, he will chuckle in memory and, doubtless, will thank heaven again for a lesson well learned in his childhood.

In the July, 1970, *Guideposts,* our widely respected TV News commentator, Walter Cronkite, tells interestingly of when and how he learned the importance and significance of honesty. For those who did not read the article, here is a gist.:

Once, when I was a boy, I saw a dollar Ingersoll watch in the showcase of our local druggist. I wanted that watch very much but didn't have the dollar; so, I asked the druggist if I could take it and then pay for it as I earned the money. He agreed. The next day my mother happened to come into the store, and the druggist casually mentioned the arrangement we had made.

Well, my parents would have none of it. To them what I had done was the next thing to dishonesty.

"Don't you see," my mother said to me, "you already consider the watch yours but you haven't paid for it. That's deception. If you have to use the slightest bit of dishonesty to get what you want, you're paying too high a price."

She paid the druggist a dollar, took the watch from me and kept it until I earned the money to retrieve it.

Concerning the impact of that lesson, Mr. Cronkite said:

That lesson has stuck with me. Today I have almost a compulsive desire to be honest, not because I think it makes me any better than the next man, but because I feel so strongly about the need for honesty in our national life. If we want to see straight dealing in our country, the place to begin is with ourselves.[3]

A Special Problem

At the time of the composition of this chapter, a larger-than-usual number of cases of teen-age shoplifting occurred with resultant news items in local papers. One mother, whose daughter and other girls, all from families of good economic status, had been caught in shoplifting, wrote to Columnist Abigail Van Buren to tell of her sorrow. A part of Abby's reply gave these rules for parents to establish to curb shoplifting:

1. Explain to your youngsters that shoplifting is a CRIME, which leaves a criminal record. And a lifetime record is a lifetime shadow.
2. Emphasize that going along with the crowd for fear of being 'chicken' is the coward's way out.
3. When youngsters go on a shopping expedition, know where your child is going, how much money he has, and what he expects to buy.
4. If your child comes home with more merchandise than he or she had money to buy, ask about it, and don't take any easy answers about where it came from.
5. If your daughter goes shopping with an oversize purse, be wary.
6. Outlaw all clothes swapping unless the parents on both sides know what is being exchanged.
7. Practice what you preach.[4]

"But Mother . . . Daddy!"

And when you have taught by both example and precept and have applied the precepts to everyday situations, be not surprised that son or daughter interjects with displeasure, "But, Mother . . . Daddy, other parents don't look at it that way. Let me tell you what Billy's daddy told him one day."

In some instances, Billy may have been trying to make his dad look like a daring male and, in a false sense of how to build up the image of his dad, stretched or misinterpreted an episode. Children have been known to do that! On the other hand, Billy may be telling the truth, sad as that is.

Regardless of the "But, Mother . . . Daddy" insistence of youngsters, honest parents are honor-bound to stick by what they know to be honest, and they are correct in insisting that their children do so, also. Despite the temporary disappointment of a child whose desires have been temporarily frustrated, that child, grown up into manhood and womanhood, will look back as Walter Cronkite and a host of others do and will say, "Thank God that my parents had the courage to be honest, the consistency to teach their children honesty, and to insist that the children obey." It may be a long time coming, but that statement will come, and it will be worth waiting for!

"As the Crow Flies"

When I was a preschool child, I sat often alongside my grandfather, a venerable and knowledgeable citizen of his area. Often early-day travelers, traveling over what was an unmarked trail, would pause at the front gate to ask the distance to the next town. Unerringly, my grandfather would reply, "Well, as the crow flies, it's exactly nine miles." Having been taught not to question my grandfather when he was in conversation with someone else, I did not ask what the crow's flight had to do with the distance; and, by the time the inquirer had departed, the question had disappeared in a little boy's wonderment at the car being driven by the traveler.

Later, the meaning of "as the crow flies" came to be clear. Grandfather was saying, simply: "Well, if you stay on that winding road, it will be twelve miles. If you board the nearby train, it will be ten miles. But, now if you want to know the exact distance—the honest distance, the distance as the crow would fly it, it is only nine miles. Now, many years later, there is a ribbon of concrete stretching between the two towns; and, can you guess it? The distance, clocked often on my car, is exactly nine miles!

If parents can so live and teach their children to live their lives as the crow flies his flight—thinking, speaking, and doing the honest thing—they will have given to them a life-enriching and a life-strengthening principle. Regardless of the worsening nature of society in this regard, and regardless of the "But, Mother . . . Daddy" interjections, parents who want to give their children the great basic, indispensable principle for happiness and abiding success will live and teach honesty day and night, year after year, consistently, courageously, eternally!

5

Parents Teaching . . .

Sex: Gift with a Purpose

Doubtless, to most parents the two most terrifying discoveries concerning their teen-agers are drug use and premarital pregnancy, both of which discoveries are made by multiple thousands of parents each year. Even if parents have done their best through good communication and faithful teaching, there is heartache in either discovery; but parents who have not done their best to prepare their children to eschew drug use and premarital sex should feel both heartache and remorse.

In the matter of sex, surely, parents must be aware that some corner newsstands with their paperback books, some magazines on the same stands, readily accessible "boot-legged" sex magazines, the flashing signs of many movies, and the abundant conversations among youngsters bombard their children with dangerous presentations. The nudism, the perversions, and the increasing impression that sex-outside-of-marriage is acceptable are presented with cleverness.

Therefore, to wise parents the question is not "Shall we provide our children with sex information and instruction?" but "What are the best procedures to help our children to have a wholesome knowledge of the God-intended purpose of sex—even prior to their teen years?"

I often wonder how there can still be parents with eyes to see and ears to hear who contend that sex instruction is unnecessary, that children will "find out in the normal growth process, and that instruction in the meaning and purpose of sex will just over-stimulate their interest!" As late as the spring of 1970 an adult in a church in which I was speaking protested to the pastor that the visiting speaker should not discuss sex in answer to frank questions from young people in the church (in a youth seminar). The adult's contention was that if there were no discussion of sex, there would be no problems in that area!

I contend that if sex is discussed in the light of its *purpose,* the possibility of its abuse and misuse will be greatly diminished. *The clear purpose of God's gift of sex to men and women is that it is exclusively a privilege of marriage, to be prepared for intelligently in advance of marriage, but to be experienced only after the two have been united in the holiness of marriage.* Taught with that ideal bright, clear, and unmistakable, sex instruction becomes a wise answer to the normal curiosity of growing children and can protect those children from the dirty, nauseous approaches to which they are sure to be submitted in their teen years.

Whence the Instruction?

Insofar as wholesome approaches are concerned, the three institutions which touch most young people are school, church, and home. Is it wise for the school and church to do any instruction in sex, or should they merely supplement the home, or should the home commit *all* of the instruction to church and school? A look into the possibilities of school and church approaches now and a later look into the home as the source of instruction will be profitable.

The school.—A furious tempest has raged in many sections of our nation concerning sex instruction in public schools, and the issue is far from settled. Many educators and parents argue strongly for such instruction; some other educators, some religious leaders, and many parents argue strongly against it; with fear of adding another controversy to the problems already at hand, most schools have not undertaken any definite programs of sex instruction.

Dr. Alan F. Guttmacher, M.D., president of Planned Parenthood-World Population, contends for sex instruction in the schools and suggests that the definite instruction come in grades 5, 8, and 11, but he adds this injunction: "No teaching would be complete unless it spelled out a code of responsible sexual behaviour . . . but it is much more likely to be responsible behaviour if it is based on sound knowledge and healthy attitudes." [1]

Those who argue against sex instruction in the schools use one or more of these contentions: (1) sex instruction is exclusively a responsibility of the home; (2) the films and illustrations used in school instruction are too open, revealing, and frank; (3) school instruction answers questions the student has not asked; (4) some instructors in the courses are inclined to want to shock the students with a too-raw presentation; (5) some instructors fail to make clear that the privilege of sexual intercourse is for marriage and for marriage only.

If sex instruction is to be offered in the schools, your author feels that parents have the right to be fully advised on these points if the instruction is to be formal—as in classes:

1. What will be the content of the courses? What books, charts, and films will be used? What will be the scope of instruction?

2. Who will do the teaching? What preparation have the instructors had to prepare themselves? What is the nature of the stability of the person or persons who will teach?

3. Will the instruction make clear to the students that sexual intercourse is a privilege exclusively of marriage, and that premarital sex experiences are morally wrong and will mar the beauty and wholesomeness of the experience?

These three inquiries of parents can wisely be discussed openly and freely in called meetings of educators and parents; and, if possible and practical, the materials to be used can be shared with parents in advance, the instructors can be introduced for dialogues with the parents, and agreement can be made that the whole matter of sex instruction in the schools will be evaluated by parent-school discussions at the conclusion of the first semester of the first session.

An alternative to formal sex instruction in the schools is the possibility of having a time or times of informal instruction in assembly panels, through occasional lectures, and in adult-guided discussions in student clubs.

I have conducted many Character Emphasis Weeks in high schools, in the process of which I use the question box approach to student problems. The students are invited to drop their unsigned questions into a conveniently-placed box; and, from the second morning forward, the questions constitute the main basis of the talks to the students. Many frank questions concerning sex —particularly premarital sex—come into the boxes. On the third or fourth morning of the week, I spend the entire assembly period in answering those questions. I give the biblical and legal reasons for waiting, moving then into sociological and psychological reasons for waiting, using illustrations from life.

If parents are not giving instruction in this highly volatile area of the lives of their youngsters, why should they reprove the schools for undertaking a responsibility neglected by so many parents?

The Church.—The church has encountered some of the same opposition in the matter of sex instruction which public schools have experienced; yet, viewing the widespread sex freedom which young people are practicing, and feeling a heavy responsibility to help young people to understand the God-intended purpose of sex, some denominational groups are approaching the matter through lesson materials and through magazines designed for youth reading. Many local churches plan for helpful seminars, panels, and studies in after-church youth meetings and in youth retreats.

With the same frankness of discussion with parents in advance of the use of teaching and discussion materials as was suggested in connection with public schools, churches may well explore the possibility of offering help to young people in this area; for, indeed, the need for wise sex instruction is not only indisputable it is urgently needed.[2]

One local church approached the matter in a two-fold technique. *First,* youth leaders asked teen-agers to write out frankly what their needs and questions were in the area of sex problems, indicating the degree to which they had been helped by their parents in these matters. *Second,* the youth replies were combined into a mimeographed brochure and shared with an all-parent group. With few exceptions, the parents were amazed to discover the urgency of the problem, and many were embarrassed to realize that they had not only not recognized and met their children's needs in this regard, but had earlier objected to the church's plan to help. Be it said to the credit of the parents, they authorized the church leadership immediately to bring for lectures, seminars, and counseling one of our nation's outstanding Christian lecturers, regardless of the cost involved. Not only did this lecturer stabilize the youth of the church, but helped the parents magnificently in sessions designed to equip parents for continuing counsel in this regard.

But, regardless of how much the school and church may undertake in preparing children to understand the nature and purpose of sex, it is my deep conviction that *the home* provides the very best area, atmosphere, and opportunity for wise sex instruction.

The Haven of Home

If there should be parent readers who cling to the self-excusing attitude, "Let the problem alone; leave it to nature; they'll learn soon enough," it should shock them out of their negligence to hear that practically 75 percent of 1114 students on 55 different college and university campuses indicated in a Gallup poll that they believe it not to be important to marry a virgin of either sex. Although that revelation does not necessarily mean that 75 percent of those interviewed are having premarital sex experiences, the implication, most surely, is that they would not have convictions against such experiences.[3]

These are young people recently away from their parents and homes, and evidently they came to their campuses without the conviction that chastity matters importantly; therefore, we may deduce that their homes either did no teaching concerning the Christian concept of sex morality, or that the teaching was not effectively communicated, or that personal associations of the teen-agers outside of the home were either more persuasive or more respected than those of the parents.

Still not convinced that sex instruction in the home is of urgent importance? Perhaps hesitating parents need to know that people in position to know from constant contact with the agencies which gather statistics say that there is a reliable estimate that nearly 70 percent of brides who stand at the altar annually are not virgin, and that 22.5 percent of brides who stand at the altar each year are pregnant as they stand there. The pressure to sex prior to marriage is widespread, and the home which does not try to help its youngsters to understand and to be prepared is delinquent to a tremendous need of developing children. Therefore, the question to the wise parents is not "Shall we help our children in this regard?" Rather, the questions are "When shall we begin the instruction (what age)? How shall we proceed? What are the teaching resources available to parents?"

When to Begin

A capsule reply is this: "Not too early, not too late." Perhaps you heard of the preschool lad who came running in from playtime to ask his mother, "Mother, where did I come from?" The mother, thinking that "this is the moment," sat down and gave the preschooler a minute description of the sperm, the egg, the nine months, and the birth. Emotionally exhausted from the explanation, she asked hopefully, "Now, does that answer your question, Son?" Somewhat bewildered, the lad replied: "Well my play-buddy told me he came from Indianapolis, and I just wanted to know where I came from." This was evidently a too-early journey into the field of sex instruction!

But a greater danger is the "too late" attempt. Another intriguing episode tells of the sixth-grade boy who told his mother, "Mom, we've been asked to write a paragraph in physiology class on where we came from. Where did I come from?"

"Your dad is in the den, Son; go ask him," replied the mother. The boy related the same information and request to his dad, who had not bothered to prepare either the boy or himself to help the boy in sex knowledge, and his dad replied, "Your granddad is in the living room, Son; go ask him."

The youngster found his granddad, related his need, and repeated the question, "Where did I come from?" The granddad had the answer immediately: "Why, the stork brought you, Son."

"Where did Dad come from?" continued the boy. "The stork brought him, too," replied the granddad. "Well, where did you come from, Granddad?" pressed the sixth grader. "The stork brought me, too," declared the grandparent.

In his paragraph for the physiology class the next day the boy wrote: "There has not been a normal birth in my family for three generations!" Evidently his parents had waited too late!

Children vary in the ages at which they ask their first questions concerning the sex areas of their own bodies or questions concerning how life begins. The discerning parent will be able to discover from a child's curiosity, and from his questions *when* that time has arrived.

Friends of mine welcomed, first, a little daughter. When she was four years of age, a little brother arrived. As the four-year-old daughter observed the daily bath for the new arrival, she noticed immediately the difference between his body and hers and wanted to know "Why?" The couple made a wise decision immediately—they would answer her questions unhurriedly, in a normal voice, sitting down in most instances to share the impression that they were available for any conversation concerning that matter. When they had answered her questions in language appropriate to her age and vocabulary, they said: "Now, dear, when you want to ask questions or to talk about that portion of your body, be sure to come to Mother and Dad. We are always willing to answer our little girl's questions."

In that open, unhurried, unwhispered attitude they established a bridge between themselves and the daughter, and she crossed that bridge often as she came in from playtimes with neighborhood children, from junior high school days, and from senior high sharings of her peers. She attended a university of more than 20,000 students, faced all of the loose sex talk and action of a contemporary campus, but she would have died before being immoral in sex. She had long known its purpose and was never tempted by her own emotions to betray that knowledge.

From early showering with his two sons, this same professional man found that the questions came; and as he and the boys golfed, skiied, hunted, and fished together, there were many times of frank and easy discussions between the boys and the man they respected above all others.

When to begin? At whatever time the discerning parent feels that the child is wondering about his body, its difference from the opposite sex, or how life begins.

How to Proceed

The *Minneapolis Tribune* carried a series of articles[4] concerning sex education, reporting the counsel of a group of experts in the field of sex education, all of them parents with experience in answering the questions of their children. While pointing out that the variation in children may mean that some will ask questions of their own quite early, the time to begin direct sex education is at two years of age. In counseling *how to proceed,* they stressed such matters as these: (1) Use plain talk, not trying to be poetic, designating parts of the body by their correct names; (2) Be honest, telling the child correctly what you do know, admitting that you do not know if you do not, offering to search with him or her for the correct answer; (3) Say "we'll discuss that later" if a question is asked in a company or situation in which a better discussion can be had otherwise—and making sure to talk about it later; (4) Maintain an attitude which makes it easy for children to ask again and again as they develop; (5) Don't overanswer a child's question on sex as if a whole lifetime of information must be given at once; satisfy his quest at that time, and wait for later questions.

Teaching Resource for Parents

The resources available to parents for sex instruction are, primarily, of two types: (1) everyday or neighborhood circumstances, and (2) printed materials.

In the "everyday or neighborhood circumstances" are such possibilities as these: the birth process of animal pets in or around the household, the pregnancy and birth of a baby to neighbors, or a similar experience in one's own household if there is more than one child in the family. There are many parents who use these close-to-the-child experiences to explain the origin of life, from which explanation it is comparatively easy to move on to explanations of the importance of exercising the sex privilege only in marriage. Some parents have reported to me that the earlier the average child understands the birth experience, the less he is interested in the whispered half-truths of his peers, and the more normal the matter of birth becomes to his thinking. To this normalcy of feeling concerning the "mystery" of sex, these parents have added fully, convincingly, and winsomely the reasons for waiting for marriage in the matter of sex. In no instance in these families have there been any teen-age problems in sex, and their children have a sense of pride, appreciation, and deep respect for their parents. One sixteen-year-old from one of these families came home from school one day and said with evident disgust: "The limited, silly, wrong information so many of my friends have about sex is amazing. Mom and Dad, don't think that I'm not everlastingly grateful to you for helping me to know the truth about sex."

Printed Materials

No parent needs to feel panic-stricken concerning "Where in the world can I find information for my children and information concerning proper approaches of instruction?" The materials are available in abundance and easily accessible today.

The printed volumes available to assist parents for their own knowledge as instructors and for placing in the hands of their children are now numerous, and the number increases each year. Therefore, it behooves the parents with several children to review the available volumes in book shops—particularly, religious book shops—periodically; or, if no book shop is available locally, to ask for catalogs of available recommended books by writing to such book stores. Also, book sections in newspapers and magazines may be scanned for possible new books in the area of sex instruction.

In the resource or book list chapter of this volume parents will find my list of some of the best books currently available for for parents and children, listed under the heading, "Sex Instruction" in the book list. Although I do not imply that these are necessarily the best, and, surely not the only books highly recommended in the list, I do wish to call attention here to just a few of these books (information concerning publisher may be found in the book list):

1. Concordia Press has prepared a series of paperback volumes with these titles: *I Wonder, I Wonder, Wonderfully Made, Take The High Road, Life Can Be Sexual, Parents' Guide To Christian Conversation About Sex, Christian Views Of Sex Education.*

2. A reasonably new four-volume series *The Life Cycle Library*

is now available. In addition to the four volumes to be put in the hands of the children, there is an additional volume, *Parents Answer Book,* which provides answers which parents can use in answering the 100 questions which children ask most frequently. A dedicated mother of five children reports that, after examining the four volumes for children, she placed them with confidence in the hands of the children. Her concluding statement is this: "It makes the responsibility of sex education in the home so much easier." [5]

3. Some remarkably fine and useful books have been prepared by Dr. Evelyn Millis Duvall, who is an intelligent, well-informed Christian writer. You will find these books listed in the resource or book list at the conclusion of this volume.

4. In addition to books mentioned above, two other helpful works for parents' use in preparing to teach their children are these: (1) *Teaching About Sex,* by John Howell, and (2) *How To Tell Your Child About Sex,* by James D. Hymes, Jr. *Reminder:* Full information concerning the publishers and addresses are given in the resource or book list at the conclusion of this volume.

Pamphlets, Too

In addition to the many books now available, there are most helpful pamphlets obtainable. Two sources for such pamphlets are listed here:

1. The American Institute of Family Relations (5287 Sunset Boulevard, Los Angeles, California, 90027) publishes a fine variety of pamphlets, priced from 10¢ upward. Just a few titles useful in sex instruction are these: "Building Sex Into Your Life," "Are Virgins Out Of Date?," "Dating Do's And Don'ts," "Why Aren't Boys Told These Things?," "Your Son At Seventeen," "If Your Daughter Pets," "Why Are Fathers Failures?" "Some Basic Principles Concerning Sex Education For Your Children," and many others.

2. Public Affairs Pamphlets offer a tremendous variety of brief, but helpful discussions on aspects of life and personality, including sex and sex instruction. Specific titles and per pamphlet prices can be obtained by writing to Public Affairs Pamphlets, 381 Park Avenue, South, New York, N.Y., 10016.

To Guide or Not to Guide?

While recognizing that sex instruction involves a delicacy not involved in most other discussions of parents with children, we must recognize, too, that the deadliest influences ever at work in our nation are intent on leading young people to discard the clear injunctions of God's Word concerning sex-saved-for-marriage. Therefore, parents must choose: *Shall we prepare ourselves to counsel winsomely, intelligently with our children concerning this truly wonderful—and, if wisely developed, controlled, and saved for marriage, truly beautiful—power with which God has endowed them? Or shall we "leave it to others," hopeful that our children will learn the truth?*

We are obliged to remember that the "others" who may do the teaching may well include the worst possible influences and not necessarily the completely wholesome influences which the home *can* provide in parent-guided sex instruction. At best, the hit-and-miss sources of sex information outside the home are not adequate and rarely, if ever, given in the framework of love and concern.

I believe that the parents who are committed to preparing their children for the loftiest of ideals in living will choose *home* as the site and atmosphere for sex education, and that they will prepare themselves to be the teachers in that important area in which their children need knowledge and wisdom. And, regardless of the reaction of the children as they grow up, they will eventually rise to call their parents "blessed"!

6

Parents Teaching . . .

Three Hazards: Drugs, Alcohol, Tobacco

On the same day on which this chapter was begun, the news media announced that two teen-age sons of two very prominent families were escorted to juvenile court by their parents to face charges of forbidden drug possession. Ten other young persons of less notable parentage were in the same court on similar charges, reported a news article, *and twenty-four adults were in the same court that day on charges ranging from selling heroin to being present when illegal drugs were being used.*

That episode occurred in just one city in one court day. When we recall that, throughout our nation, similar scenes were occurring in court chambers, we are made aware again of the widespread nature of the problem of drug abuse, and of some adult involvement in the sale and tacit endorsement of drug abuse, and that the drug hazard is not merely a hallmark of escape attempts by young people of poverty backgrounds or difficult ethnic problems, but that the hazard has reached its deadly grasp into families of economic, social, and educational advantage.

Scope of the Problem

While surveys and estimates concerning the scope of the drug use problem among young people vary—both according to individual surveys and individual areas surveyed, all knowledgeable authorities agree that the problem is distressingly widespread. One survey of 4,509 students in 39 schools reported this finding:

> The average youthful drug user is more likely to have a $10 weekly allowance than a $2 one. His father is more likely to be a professional man than a clerk. And he probably gets poorer marks in school than a non-user.
>
> Also, there's a better chance the young narcotics experimenter will be a boy rather than a girl, have a father who uses tobacco and alcohol, and parents without religious affiliation.[1]

While, as the above survey indicated, children of nonchurch families have a higher incidence of drug use, it is heartbreaking to discover that a significant number of youthful drug users do have parents who are active in religious affiliations. Therefore, even active church parents must be aware that they, too, need to be alert to the drug menace to their children and must do everything possible to prepare their youngsters to resist the many opportunities to experiment with the dangerous drugs.

Why Do They Do It?

In answering the foregoing question, one writer said:

> The reasons behind this question are almost as legion as the personalities behind them. Youth have cited the following reasons for taking drugs: It is "in", to see what it is like (curiosity), a dare (social pressure), peer acceptance, to escape from reality, to find themselves, to relieve inhibitions, to get away from something, for something to do, to relieve tension and anxiety, to relieve feelings of inadequacy, because they are unhappy with society, instability of their lives, curiosity about their inner thoughts, to take a chance.[2]

The same author points out that the "pill happy" society of which the teen-ager is a part must bear a large responsibility for the teen-ager's curiosity about the effect of drugs and for his desire to "see what happens." Instead of blaming peer group pressure as the main "recruiter" of young people to drug using, he says: "If we are trying to locate the culprit responsible for the increase of drug abuse among our youth, then we had better look at the society which has created such an atmosphere that spawns such behavior."[3]

At the time of the composition of this chapter, I saw a penetrating cartoon in a daily newspaper. In the cartoon, an adult was being carried, lying down, by eight characters in bottle or pillbox body forms, each with a label of an adult-taken drug ("Drugs to pep you up, Drugs to calm you down, Drugs to go to sleep, Drugs to stay awake, Alcohol, Cigarettes, etc."). The adult being borne by the sustaining "army" of his own drugs was reading a newspaper and exclaiming, "Kids On Dope? Where Do They Get Those Wild Ideas?"[4]

A Federal Source Book: Answers To The Most Frequently Asked Questions About Drug Abuse suggests these as possible reasons for youth's use of drugs:

1. The widespread belief that "medicines" can magically solve problems.
2. The numbers of young people who are dissatisfied or disillusioned or who have lost faith in the prevailing social system.
3. The tendency of persons with psychological problems to seek easy solutions with chemicals.
4. The easy access to drugs of various sorts.
5. The development of an affluent society that can afford drugs.
6. The statements of proselyters who proclaim the "goodness" of drugs.[5]

Although I have not made a special study of drug use among teen-agers, nor have I counseled with as many of them as have so many authorites in the field, from my contacts, observations, and conversations with parents and counselors, I feel that these are the principal reasons for youth's beginning to experiment with drugs.

1. *Immaturity,* which keeps him from looking at the eventual result of a practice which, meanwhile, may lead him to feel that he will

be a "hero" to drug-using peers if he can report "how much I can stand."

2. *Insecurity,* which gives him the desire to explore an experience which, while it lasts, may give him a feeling of security.

3. *Fears* of a hundred kinds concerning himself, his adequacy for life, his family, his acceptance by friends, *ad infinitum* may lead him to drugs in a desperate desire to be relieved, even if temporarily, from fear.

4. *Frustrations* in efforts, activities, attempts at acceptance could produce a desire to escape into an imaginary world of achievement.

5. *Maladjustment* of any sort—physical, mental, family, social, spiritual —and the resultant desire to "get away from it all" could impel the youth to try drugs.

6. *Home Tensions* between parents, between himself and parents, between himself and brothers or sisters or other relatives could mislead a young person into a desire for escapism into the euphoria temporarily provided by some drugs.

7. *Hostilities* toward parents, teachers, school generally, church, society, and a desire to "show them" or hurt them could lead to drug use.

8. *Peer Pressure* of exactly the same sort which leads many young people to take a first cigarette or a first drink of liquor is responsible for some beginnings to experiment with drugs. The feeling, "Nothing can hook me; I can stop it when I want to," deludes many young people, doubtless, into their first succumbings to peer pressure.

9. *Poor Motivation*—no specific goals, no vocational choice, no achievements worthy of notice by others, and even a "nothing to live for" lethargy impels some to the drug use habit.

10. *Misinformation* concerning the hurt of some drugs and the danger of addiction is responsible for some youth beginnings of drug use. When people in positions of apparent knowledge and influence advocate the legalization of marijuana, for instance, despite the indisputable medical advice which indicates its deleterious effects upon users, young people "grab" the advocacy of marijuana as sure proof that it is not dangerous. From their own peers, also, they often receive such misinformation.

What Can Parents Do?

1. Parents can make sure that they are as fully advised as pos-

sible concerning (1) the nature and types of drugs dangerous for use, (2) the habits of the close associates of their children, and (3) the symptoms of drug abuse.

Nature and types of drugs may be learned easily by reference to any number of excellent booklets of information available to parents. In the resource or book list section of this volume under the heading of "Drugs—Liquor—Tobacco" one can find a fuller list, but here are two good reference books easily obtainable:

Drug Abuse: Teenage Hangup, written by Dr. Donald J. Merki, and available on order from TANE (Texas Alcohol Narcotics Education, Inc.) 2814 Oak Lawn Avenue, Dallas, Texas, 75219. The current cost of this excellent volume is $1.50. It is a 138 page booklet with a wealth of information concerning the history of drug use, current problems, symptoms of drug abuse, listings and discussions of dangerous drugs, and a bibliography.

A Federal Source Book: Answers to the Most Frequently Asked Questions About Drug Abuse. This booklet is published jointly by several departments of our federal government and is obtainable at 25¢ per copy from Superintendent of Documents (Dept. D), Government Printing Office, Washington, D.C., 20402, and at a smaller per-copy charge when larger quantities are ordered—perhaps for parent groups.

It is my judgment that these and other titles listed in the book list later in this volume will give parents adequate understanding of drugs and drug abuse.

The habits of the close associations of their children may not be as easy to learn as the nature of drugs and drug abuse; yet, parents *can* find out through inquiries of persons who do know. "We never dreamed that the teeners with whom our teen-ager associated were the sort who would take drugs," is the too-late wail of many parents of our day; and some of those parents might have learned earlier if they had made intelligent inquiries.

The symptoms of drug use are not necessarily the same in all drug users, nor do the symptoms appear as readily in some individuals as in others; but one authority in discernment of drug use indicates these as general symptoms:

1. A drastic change in one's attitude toward school, friends, and other activities.
2. A shift in friendships.
3. A marked deterioration in overall personal appearance.
4. Sudden and frequent absences from school.
5. A general listlessness about life.
6. Criminal involvement—particularly theft.
7. Hypersensitivity, edgy behavior.
8. Borrowing money from people at school.
9. Observing the student in unusual isolated places around the school building.
10. Any signs of equipment that can be associated with drug abuse, such as rags, spoons, needles, tubes, aerosol cans, etc.[6]

It is obvious that an at-home parent will not be able to discern the above-named symptoms which appear chiefly at school; yet, school personnel are being sufficiently advised of these symptoms, so that they will not be reluctant to pass on to parents any well-founded observations.

2. Parents can keep in touch with the local problem. Local sources of information concerning drug abuse are some or all of these: school officials, law-enforcement agencies, newspapers, youth organizations, juvenile court officials, family counseling services, and, in some instances, special groups which have been organized to study the problem locally.

3. Parents can place information concerning drugs and their dangers in the hands of their children. Several of the items which readers will find listed in the resource-book list at the conclusion of this volume are written with youth readers in mind. In addition to booklets and pamphlets, TANE (mentioned above) publishes a clever disc, titled Dial-a-Drug, and it is produced primarily for youth perusal. There is a "pie-section" portion cut out of the top and bottom layers of the disc, so that, as the young person turns this cut-out portion, he sees revealed on the middle disc complete information concerning one drug: its legal names (if legal), its slang name, its medical classification and uses (if any), the symp-

toms of abusers, its form-taste-smell, route of administration (ingested, sniffed, etc.), whether or not it is legal, and the penalty for illegal possession. *And all this information is available on the two sides of the disc concerning sixteen prevalent drug types.* Along with the disc, TANE sends a Dial-a-Drug booklet which is useful for parents, teachers, and students. It contains a wealth of information most attractively presented.

4. Parents can support school, church, and community efforts which seek to inform young people of this menace and to give them courage to resist.

5. Parents can keep channels of communication concerning the drug problem open between themselves and their childrem—perhaps through joint study of the materials mentioned and through continuing discussions as occasions and incidents arise.

In addition to the foregoing ways in which the parent can help, *A Federal Source Book,* mentioned above, offers these suggestions (numbers used below are the numbers of these suggestions in *A Federal Source Book*):

6. "He (the parent) can set a good example by not abusing drugs himself. Since he can expect his children to model their drug-taking behavior after his, he can either refrain from drinking socially or drink in moderation." (Author's note: In my judgment, gleaned from many years of counseling, *only total abstinence on the parent's part is a safe example!*)

7. "Most important of all, he can strive to meet the ideals of parenthood, trying to rear his children so that they are neither deprived of affection or spoiled. He should have a set of realistic expectations for them. He should give his children responsibilities according to their capabilities, and not overprotect them from the difficulties they will encounter. A parent should be able to talk frankly with his children, and they to him." [7]

If It Happens!

But if, after all a good parent has done, a child in the family is involved in drug abuse, what should the parent do? Quite naturally, the situation will depend upon whether or not the youthful drug-user has yet fallen into the hands of the law. If he has not, there are family procedures recommended for both the youngster wanting to be helped and the one who is hostile and has no desire to stop drug use. If he has fallen into the hands of the law, parents will receive some counsel from the courts; and, in either case—family handling or court-handling—there are counseling programs for both parents and youth in almost all of our urban centers.

Instead of going into detail with the problems facing parents who find children to be drug-users, I recommend strongly that concerned parents do two things:

1. That they consult immediately with their family physicians, asking their judgment as to the medical problem, legal aspects as related to the problem, and that they consult the counseling sources recommended.

2. That they obtain copies of two publications mentioned above: (1) *Drug Abuse: Teenage Hangup* from TANE (address given both above and in the book list at the conclusion of this volume) for the important chapter, "Treatment and Rehabilitation: The Road Back"; (2) *A Federal Source Book* (also mentioned above with proper address, and in the book list) for guidance on pages 4 and 5. If your church library does not have these volumes, why not urge that they be obtained, thereby making them available immediately if needed by distressed parents?

Repetition for Emphasis

Parents will be wise to review honestly their own "addictions" to legal drugs; for, if youngsters find a great variety of pep pills, tranquilizers, sedatives, and the like in parents' medicine cabinets and are aware that their parents are using legally dispensed drugs excessively, their immaturity may well lead them to ask, "Well, why shouldn't *I* have my drug supply, since Mom and Dad have theirs?"

And Mom and Dad have theirs, according to reliable statistics! The Commissioner of the Food And Drug Administration has only recently accused the pharmaceutical manufacturers of actually fostering the use and abuse of "pep pills" through overproduction —three and a half billion amphetamine pills and tablets in our country in 1969, which, as the Commissioner pointed out, is a much larger quantity than the medical needs of our nation required. Proof of the illegal diversion of much of this product is found in the statistics of the Justice Department's narcotics and dangerous drugs bureau: it was unable to account for the sale of 38 percent of the amphetamines produced during 1969! It is a safe estimate that the large majority of the legally sold pills went to adults, and that not all of the 38 percent went to youth.

Venturesome teeners of "pill popping" parents do not necessarily stop to remind themselves that their parents obtained those excessively used drugs legally: they are looking for *alibis,* not reasons. The responsible parent, therefore, will ask himself-herself: *Does my use of drugs, however legally obtained, provide an alibi for a child in my family, on the basis of which he may seek to justify his indiscriminate and, perhaps, illegal use of them?*

Liquor a Menace, Too!

In our nation's recent preoccupation with the problem of drugs, we have failed to remind ourselves that liquor drinking has actually become a bigger problem than narcotics addiction in its quantitative scope and in its toll of human strength, happiness, and even life. Although United Nations studies, a few ignored voices in the chambers of Congress, and local surveys of teen-age drinking continue to remind us of the desperate toll which this addiction exacts from our nation, its social acceptability and, sad to say, the fact that it makes money for dealers and produces taxes for all levels of government have largely stilled our tongues and have caused legislatures and Congress to decline to require even the warnings which cigarette packages must carry!

Teen-agers, Too?

There is no adult indulgence of dangerous nature in our nation which is as tragically reflected in teen-age life as the drink habit. With five to six million alcoholics, with several million more of adults getting closer to addiction, and with still others in the social drinking class, is it surprising that surveys of some junior and senior high school students in several of our cities come up with the information that a very high percentage of young people drink? A survey of high school students in one of our Southern cities revealed not only a high percentage of student drinkers, but that they did not have much difficulty obtaining the beverages in restaurants and even from liquor stores, despite their being under legal age and that many of the teen drinkers indicated that they had no difficulty in finding liquor in their own homes.[8]

Why?

Some of the reasons for teen-age drinking are the same as their reasons for experimenting with drugs:

1. *Peer pressure* is a large factor. In the survey of high school students, referred to above, most of the students replied to the question, "Why?," with such replies as "Everybody does it . . . Just to keep up with the crowd, I guess . . . I don't know why: I just do."

2. *High social acceptability* of drinking in our nation with no illegal implications (as in drugs) leads many young people to assume that drinking is completely acceptable.

3. *The glamour of advertising alcoholic beverages* leads many young people to think that it is a sophisticated habit, associated with "the good life."

4. *Psychological difficulties*—fear, frustration, insecurity, and similar upsetting factors lead at least a few young people to use liquor as an escape mechanism.

5. *Experimentation*—"to see the feeling or result"—induces some young people to try alcoholic beverages.

6. *Home tensions,* in the handling of which the young drinker may be simply following the example of parents in their reaction to tensions!
7. *Parental example and, tragic to say, occasional parental encouragement.* In the survey of high school students, mentioned above, there was reported this response to the question, "Why do teen-agers begin to drink?": "Parents who don't drink and some nondrinking sons and daughters of nondrinking parents insist that most drinking teen-agers learn the habit from their own drinking parents."
8. *Hostility toward nondrinking parents if those parents have unduly antagonized the teen-ager.* There are instances, revealed by surveys and which I have discovered, in which parents have been unduly harsh with teen-agers, not establishing or maintaining any degree of communication, acting almost tyrannically toward their children, never explaining, never listening to the teener's side of any disagreement, and often levying definitely unreasonable punishment. In some of these instances teen-agers have begun to drink—both as a relief from home tensions and as a "strike back" of rebellion toward parents.

Parental Procedures

How shall parents handle the problem of drinking in relationship to the conduct of their children? These few suggestions may be added to other efforts which parents know:

1. *Clear up parental example.* It seems to me that a drinking parent's exhortations to teen-age children "not to drink" is an exercise in both hypocrisy and futility. The "sophisticated" counsel that it is wise to teach's one's children to drink moderately at home in order to prevent drinking heavily later is as illogical as counseling one's children to use dangerous drugs only moderately with the hope that they will not become addicts! Liquor *is* a narcotic, and addiction to it with all of its damage to body, mind, personality, marriage, and career is an everpresent possibility in the life of an individual who begins to drink at all. Therefore, the wise parent will make sure that he is not giving a youngster in his family any possible alibi to drink because "Mom and Dad do it."

2. *Place intelligent, scientific information in the ready reach of youngsters.* Reading the materials as parents, so as to be able to discuss them intelligently with children, will be useful. Although a fuller list of available books and pamphlets will be found in the resource-book list at the conclusion of this volume, here are four titles of excellent information, primarily slanted to youth:

Alcohol: Fun or Folly? (Lindsay R. Curtis, M.D., obtainable through TANE, listed earlier in this chapter and again in the resource book list)
Alcohol: Your Blood and Your Brain (Lindsay R. Curtis, M.D. This excellent booklet is based upon the currently released studies of Dr. Melvin H. Knisely, portions of which were carried in the June, 1970, issue of *Reader's Digest*). This booklet is obtainable from TANE, also.
The Many Faces of Ethyl (William S. Garmon, Broadman Press, 127 Ninth Avenue, North, Nashville. Obtainable, also, in book stores)
Alcohol Today: a Workbook for Youth (By Bill Bailey. This is a two-color study guide and workbook for junior and senior high school students and is obtainable from TANE, whose address is found both in the Drug section of this chapter and in the resource-book list).

3. *Encourage study groups, seminars, panels for youth in your church.* With much excellent material available and with a growing number of adults who have convictions sufficient to enable them to conduct these groups, such groups would serve two excellent purposes: (1) They would give splendid, intelligent, scientific reasons for not drinking—reasons which teeners can use proudly in explaining why they do not drink, and (2) such groups could result in the formulation of a youth group of nondrinkers; and, since teen-agers need the support and approval of a peer group, this will make possible such a group—and even the possibility that the example and influence of such a group could influence an entire high school constituency to see that it's much smarter *not* to drink.

4. *Keep an alert eye and ear for testimonies which will reenforce the importance of not drinking.* These appear occasionally in newspapers, magazines, pamphlets from doctors and other scientists, often giving the experiences of individuals in either not drinking

at all or in discovering the tragedy of drinking. These items can carry a validity of proof which will be either more effective than parental instruction alone or a deepening of the impression which parental teaching makes.

A sustaining reminder to parents to do their best to save their children from drink damage is this: *Since alcohol can damage the body, destroy brain cells, handicap the personality, ruin the marriage, wreck the career, and make a highway murderer of my children, I must do my very best through example, teaching, and encouragement to lead my children not to drink at all. I believe that if I can help them know all the valid reasons for not drinking, if I can help them to take the long look at the ultimate damage of drink, and can help them to see that, despite much society emphasis upon the "sophistication and smartness' of drinking, it is infinitely smarter not to drink, I shall have done everything possible for a parent to do. Having done that, I shall have the right to ask God to extend my efforts in ways beyond my ability to help.*

And Tobacco

Fortunately, so much medical research and its publicity have been available to the public, that the "social smartness" attached to drinking has been greatly reduced if not removed from the habit of smoking. Congressional action in requiring warnings on cigarette packages and the removal of television advertising of cigarettes have sounded the danger of tobacco use "loud and clear" to both adults and teen-agers. Therefore, parents do have a larger and stronger phalanx of allies in encouraging their youngsters not to smoke than they do in encouraging them not to drink.

The same procedures recommended for parental guidance of youngsters to abstain from drinking may be followed by parents in their teaching and encouragement to abstain from tobacco use, remembering that, if the "teacher" has to pause in the teaching to exhale his or her cigarette smoke or to shake off the ashes of a smoked cigarette, the teaching will probably have little effect—unless, forsooth, the child is so disgusted with the parent's smoking habit that the disgust turns him away from the habit, or, mayhap the parent's body, stricken as a result of the habit, becomes a sad and mournful warning!

If from discussion groups, seminars, or panels on cigarette use a movement promoted by the teen-agers themselves can develop, its effectiveness can be phenomenal. *Teen Magazine* in its June, 1969, issue shared the remarkable story of such a successful effort on the part of Bakersfield, California, teen-agers in an article titled "Smoke! Choke! Croak!" With billboards, bumper stickers, radio-TV programs, decals, buttons, bookcovers, school and local newspapers as media, the teen-agers in Bakersfield have accomplished a virtual miracle in warning their peers of the dangers of smoking, and the results have been effective, not only with teeners, but with adult listeners and viewers, too.[9]

Although several excellent publications will be found in the resource-book list which concludes this volume, the federal government's publication *Cigarette Smoking and Health Characteristics,* prepared on the basis of household interviews by the Health, Education, and Welfare Department, has a wealth of information concerning the relationship of cigarette smoking to a wide variety of physical conditions. This booklet may be obtained from Superintendent of Documents, Government Printing Office, Washington, D.C., and the current charge is only 45 cents.

If, as the frequent TV inserts repeat, youngsters can be persuaded that "it's a matter of life and breath," the addiction to tobacco may well be prevented.

7

Discipline: Meaning, Significance, Spirit

Last year columnist Ann Landers published a letter from a high school senior who was asking: "How can I get my mother to be more strict?" She was actually jealous of her friends whose mothers were firm in what they expected. Miss Lander sympathized: "You have been incapacitated by a mother who thought she was doing you a favor by making life easy and convenient."

In the same month a syndicated cartoon told it like this: in the upper panel, a father and mother were pictured in the act of reading a child guidance book which advocated permissive behavior, their infant child pictured nearby; in the lower panel the infant, now grown up on the diet of permissive behavior, was pictured in all of the appearances and implications of rebellion, disrespect, and vulgarity—to the amazement of parents and society!

At the same time, the newspapers carried a picture of a distinguished professor in an Eastern university in the act of "clobbering" with the university mace a protesting student who tried to interrupt the graduation proceedings, the implication being that if the protester had been properly disciplined in his growing-up days, he would not have needed the rather vigorous treatment accorded by the professor.

Many Voices

Opinions on discipline ranged all the way from that of the lecturer who opined that any kind of corporal punishment serves

76

only to allay the parent's anger and indicates a character break-down of the parent, to the vigorous opinion of a parent who declared that the rule without the rod is powerless.

A survey of parents in two eastern and two western states con-cerning remedies for keeping children from "running wild" re-vealed tremendous emphasis upon the need for better home discipline and factors involved in that discipline: *clear and re-peated teaching of fundamental values,* emphasis upon decency of behavior, respect for law and the rights of other people, whole-some homelife, good parental examples, strictness and consistency of administering rules, good communication between parents and children, making clear the authority of parents, spending all needed time with children in companionship. Throughout the survey there was the refrain: "Regardless of the necessity and seriousness of discipline, always make clear that there is great love for the child."[1]

The Need for Discipline

From both adults and teen-agers there is a delightfully har-monious conviction that discipline is an important even urgent need in the wholesome growing-up process; and another point of agreement between those two groups is that the parents must assume responsibility for discipline.

A British school mistress, famous for her "gentle, but firm dis-cipline with lots of love and affection" deplored in a 1970 inter-view the failure of adults to tell children their faults and who fawn over them. "Why are we afraid to tell them what we think? Instead of putting them in their place, we just lick their boots and allow them to run completely over us," this headmistress of a girls' school declared.[2]

A city council in Michigan recently passed legislation under which "parents may be jailed or fined for negligence if such negligence contributes to criminal acts committed by their chil-dren (those under 17)." Already the legislation has had several salutary effects. Many parents are taking their parenthood more responsibly, many teen-agers are thinking twice about possible capers which would involve their parents in humiliating court appearances, many families are reevaluating the parent-child relationships, and a new sense of mutual respect, love, and care seems to be developing.[3]

In midsummer of 1970, Associated Press carried an intriguing article titled "Human Parents Should Take Tip From Animals." Dr. Charles Schroeder, director of the San Diego (California) Zoo observed that "human parents trying to bring up children might take a tip from the stern disciplinarians of the animal world." He continued: "There are no juvenile delinquents in the animal world. Animal parents don't permit it."

Dr. Schroeder listed interesting episodes of instances in which animal parents, indulgent in minor ways, actually physically discipline their offspring, and he concluded his interview with these words: "But nowhere in the animal world is the offspring allowed to do as he pleases."

Youth Opinion

From a survey involving teen-agers in ten cities across our nation, Lloyd Shearer found that the teen-agers interviewed have this feeling about parents generally:

They have become too permissive, too lax, too easily defeated by an adolescent behaviour they do not understand. What they then pursue is the easy solution: the teen-ager goes his way and the parents go theirs; the teen-ager is permitted to drift, to dominate his own upbringing. Supposedly everything is fine so long as the teen-ager keeps out of trouble. Only this becomes extremely difficult for an adolescent who's been given no definite set of rules and regulations, no map to the geography of behaviour.[4]

But the picture of parental responsibility is not all dark. I found in my survey of teen-agers in twenty-one states this happy fact: in answer to the question concerning what more parents can do to help teen-agers to grow up with balance, the second largest number of suggestions indicated that their parents were doing everything possible, and the replying teen-agers felt that the rapport was excellent.

Lloyd Shearer's survey report included this inspiring section:

There are millions of teen-agers whose relationship with their parents is excellent. These teen-agers describe their parents as tolerant, reasonable, democratic, and persuasive in contrast to parents who are punitive and authoritarian. The difference between the persuasive parent who produces a useful, fairly adjusted citizen and the authoritarian who produces a rebel lies in the art of communication.

The parent who will take time to explain his rules of behaviour, his philosophy of life, his outlook on sex, his viewpoint on the use of the family car—such a parent has the best chance of nurturing an adolescent into the sort of adult he would admire and respect.[5]

And a British teen-ager whose parents are evidently the sort described with admiration in Lloyd Shearer's survey offered this interesting observation:

I'm no authority on American teen-agers, but from what I've seen I can say that they have much more freedom and much less parental supervision than we have in England. I don't think it's made them any happier or, for that matter, their parents either. It's just robbed them of their youth and taken them away from their parents. And that's sad, because parents can be fun.[6]

Therefore, we conclude from all of these many voices that discipline is not only *needed* and actually *wanted* by teen-agers, but that, also, the *responsibility* for discipline rests initially and largely upon the parents.

What Is Discipline?

In view of a wide tendency to confine the meaning of the word *discipline* to punishment, and in view of the several concepts involved in discipline, let's take a good, frank, full look at the meaning of the word and the component parts of the concept of discipline.

Encyclopaedia Britannica's excellent *Dictionary* lists six meanings, four of which are relevant to parent-child relationships:

1. "Systematic training or subjection to authority; especially in training of the mental, moral, and physical powers by instruction and exercise."
2. "The result of this (i.e. the foregoing training): subjection, habit of obedience."
3. "Training resulting from misfortunes, troubles, etc."
4. "Punishment for the sake of training: correction, chastisement."

Our English word *discipline* comes directly from the Latin word, *discipulus,* which means "disciple" or "learner." Therefore, the overriding principle in discipline is *instruction* by a teacher—in this instance, by parents. It is to be expected that this teaching-learning process will result in the child's acceptance of the principles taught, his obedience to those principles in conduct, and his understanding that obedience brings increasing esteem and the likelihood of greater trust in him, that disobedience necessitates punishment and results in damaged rapport between himself and his parents.

Component Parts of Discipline

Gleaned from surveys (my own and others), articles by both adults and teen-agers, and by personal interviews, here are some widely accepted aspects of wholesome discipline:

1. *Authority.*—the confident, positive assurance on the part of parents of what is best for the growing child in the matter of ideals and rules, and the maintenance firmly, but lovingly, of the parents' position as director of the child's behavior.

My survey of teen-agers revealed that they very much *want* their parents to be sure of their behavior guidelines and to stick by those guidelines with firmness. The insecurity of many teen-agers grows largely out of their not being sure that their parents are sure that they will actually enforce certain regulations and maintain announced limits. "I wish my parents would be firm; then I could be surer of the limits," many teen-agers have said to me.

Dr. David Edens related in a column in *Home Life* magazine that a seven-year study of the National Institutes of Mental Health revealed that young people with high self-esteem tend to come from homes with very strict parents. The study revealed, also, that those same youngsters had great success socially and academically, and that they liked and respected their positive parents. The strict parents had used rewards more than punishment to influence their children's behavior. The firm discipline of the parents in the study proved to be less degrading than the erratic punishment of permissive parents, who were neither firm regularly nor consistent in patterns of punishment.[7]

2. *Clarity and adequacy of instruction.*—Today's youngsters are growing up in a society of confusion concerning proper values; and, in many instances, they are being disillusioned by the hypocrisy of an adult society which preaches one thing and practices another. Therefore, it becomes not just desirable, but urgently imperative that parents *teach* by precept and example what the real values are. This teaching needs to be unmistakably clear concerning the application of concepts to behavior, exactly what the concepts mean, what the parents' expectations are, what the gratifications of obedience will be, and what the failure to apply the taught ideals to behavior will be. Repetition, illustration, and the sharing of reasons may be necessary to clarity and adequacy; but whatever it takes, let the instructions for wholesome living be clear and adequate.

In the clear and adequate teaching of children, many parents need to be reminded to *take the time* to be with their children in a variety of relationships, using normal situations as teaching media—playtime, leisure, shared-work times, recreational associations, for instance. The parent who is too busy to do more than to say, "Do it because I said so. I don't have time to tell you all the reasons why" is likely to produce a rebellious teen-ager, with whom he will have no rapport.

I read this item in a church bulletin:

A young man stood before a judge to be sentenced for forgery. The judge had been a great friend of the boy's father, who was famous for his books.

"Young man," said the judge sternly, "do you remember your father, that father whom you have disgraced?"

"I remember him perfectly," the young man answered quietly. "When I went to him for advice or companionship, he would say, 'Run away, boy, I am busy.' My father finished his book, and here I am."

Parents do not have the right to bring children into a world of confused and conflicting values without giving to their children a child's right to enough of a parent's time to be able to learn life's rules. Many fathers are so busy making their fame and fortune that they cheat their children of the *time* which children want and need; and many mothers permit themselves to be unnecessarily involved in money-earning and/or in self-advancing outside activities, that they shortchange their children of something for which no amount of bribes through gifts can substitute—*time* in companionship, enjoyment, and rapport, in which circumstances the very best teaching times occur.

3. *Consistency.*—In answer to my inquiry of teen-agers concerning what I should tell parents about discipline, there was a veritable chorus of suggestions amounting to this plea: "Tell parents to be consistent. They are so strict about something one time and have a 'don't care' attitude at other times. They promise certain rewards or kinds of punishment and then don't come through with what they promised or threatened. We wish we could know for sure that the limits they set are actually going to be enforced."

The best self-disciplined young man with whom I ever worked had enjoyed a wide and happy series of dating experiences in his college years, and it was supposed by many of his friends that he would go directly to the marriage license bureau upon receiving his college degree. Knowing of the young man's romantic proclivities, I asked him how he had managed to stay unwed throughout college.

"Wait 'till you come to know my parents," was his reply. When asked what he meant, he gave a revealing reply.

"My parents were completely consistent in rearing me," he said. "They never failed to do what they said they would do, be it reward or punishment. When I was on the eve of departing for college, they said to me: 'Son, we are willing to send you to college for as many degrees as you want to take, but the day you get married, you are out of the family feed trough.' Because they had always been consistent—never overstating nor understating their expectations and intentions—I knew they meant what they were saying. Since I could not possibly have supported a wife during college days, their consistent dealings with me simply removed that possible temptation."

When I asked him if he thought they might have changed their minds, had he married during college years, he replied: "No, sir, not my parents. They always made sure what was right to ask of me, and they couldn't have lived with themselves if they had not stuck by what they had discovered to be right and wise."

4. *Fair thinking and acting.*—This fairness of spirit involves a willingness to hear a child through when he seeks to explain, to give the benefit of the doubt when it is evident that a misunderstanding has occurred, not condemning the child's whole character because of a single act of wrong, criticizing the act without belittling or degrading the child, being patient to explain fully all the reasons *why* a wrong deed is wrong, giving him an opportunity to make restitution if such is in order or to voice a resolution to act differently in the future; and, if punishment is required by consistency, to suit the punishment to the act and *not* to the parent's anger or disappointment!

5. *Respect for the child.*—While maintaining authority as a parent, while being clear and adequate in instruction, and while

being completely consistent in discipline, parents need to respect the child as a person—his right to ask, to seek, to grow into an independent personality; his right to security, happiness, and self-respect. Some parents practically crush the important ego development of children by treating them as if they know nothing at all, as if they are never right in any circumstance, as if they have no right to think or decide or act except as parents direct. This is directly opposite to the parental attitude which accords a child unlimited and unguided choice in behavior, and the result to the child in either of these extremes is unfortunate and, at times, disastrous.

This respect for the child will include a respect for his need and desire for *privacy*. There are times in which developing children need to be alone with their thoughts, times in which an unwarranted intrusion of parents can be little less than "nosy" and can be so irritating to the children involved—so much so that their desire to confide in parents will be destroyed. The need for privacy will vary with children in the same family, and wise parents will discern the differing needs. One teen-ager in my survey stated the need tersely in these words: "Parents should not be so nosy about some personal things. Kids need privacy. Parents should be aware of what's going on, but, at the same time, should not insist on knowing every little detail of a youngster's life and thinking."

6. *Forgiveness.*—One teen-ager in my survey stated the need and wisdom of forgiveness from parents in these terms: "When a kid does something wrong, he should be reprimanded or punished, but after that the parent should not 'rub it in' by continuing to remind the child of his wrongdoing; and, parents, please don't tell other people 'what your dumb kid did!' "

In short, parents can well emulate the forgiving spirit of God toward *their* transgressions; for, as we remember, God not only forgives those transgressions, but remembers them against the transgressor no more! The parent who keeps reminding the child of a former wrong is placing about his neck the child's version of the Ancient Mariner's albatross, while the parent who forgives and remembers the child's wrongdoing no more *against him* is likely to help the child to love both earthly and heavenly parentage more fully and warmly.

7. *Parental example.*—In the discernment so typical of most young people, they have insisted in all of the surveys that good examples of *living* on the part of their parents have been a tremendous disciplinary factor. In the first place, the lip teaching is validated by the life living, and discerning youngsters will believe what these parents say. In the second place, while parents may wonder often if their examples are "lost" on their children, the children (teen-agers particularly) volunteer the information in surveys that the good example of parents is a powerful factor in their own decisions. Over and over again they have said, "I would die before consciously doing anything that would grieve my parents, for they have been such wonderful examples."

Still other teen-agers whose parents have not been good examples are crying out their complaints, as in Lloyd Shearer's survey:

(Some parents) are frauds, phonies, and hypocrites. . . . (You) preach one set of values and practice another. . . . You don't know what you really believe in, so how can we? . . . (Some) grownups like to say that teen-agers are rebels without a cause. That's not true. We have a cause. We want you to give us a truthful sense of values, a practical code of ethics, a code you're willing to live by as well as us.[8]

It behooves every parent to ask and answer honestly the question: In which direction is my example leading or pushing my children?

8. *Individualize parent-child relationships.*—While maintaining some standards for the entire family, parents will be wise to remember that one child may need more of explanation and repetition than others concerning both rules and wrongs, that reproof and punishment of one sort may not be the wisest for each child

in the family, that some children need more attention and assurance than others, that some children can be released to their own judgment earlier than others, and that it is generally not wise to compare one child's achievements with another—particularly to the discredit or downgrading of one child.

9. *Praise with challenge.*—All normal persons and particularly developing children actually need some degree of praise for worthy achievements. For worthy behavior, particularly obedience under difficult circumstances, praise for children is in order. However, the praise should be given in such manner as not to lull the child into the feeling that "now I can get off the reservation in some aspect of conduct," but bestowed with the unmistakable implication that the parent expects to be able to continue the approbation because of continuing good conduct.

10. *Responsibility.*—In keeping with a child's growth and development increasing responsibilities can be wisely assigned, in the performance of which responsibilities the child can learn some essential values, develop a sense of self-reliance and self-discipline, and validate in experience some of the values taught by parents.

A second type of desirable responsibility is that of the parents' passing on responsibility for good behavior to the child after the clear and adequate teaching process recommended above.

The assumption of responsibility and the successful handling of it can become the basis of justifiable pride and happiness on the part of both parent and child and can become a factor in deepening rapport and developing maturity of the parent-child relationship.

11. *Reevaluation.*—A reevaluation of rules, expectations, and understandings may well be most valuable in these instances:

a. In increasing hostilities on the part of the child toward rules and obedience. Such questions as these are in order: have we as parents been clear enough and fair enough in instructions, decisions, rewards, punishments? Is the hostility on the part of the child attributable to possible physical or mental handicaps—even

hidden handicaps—such as an unrecognized hearing or sight difficulty or a minimal neurological handicap (or minimal brain
dysfunction)? If the child is a teen-ager, is the hostility attributable
to a normal desire for growing independence?

b. In the growing-up process of the child. How much more responsibility for self-discipline should we accord the child? In what
ways do we need to change our parental techniques in dealing
with the child in discipline?

c. In some few instances in which a child (teen-ager, for instance) depends too totally upon parental guidance, not assuming
normal responsibility for decisions and actions. This circumstance
is not frequent, but it does occur. The teen-ager who leaves *all*
responsibility for every decision with parents will be poorly adjusted when he leaves home for college, military service, or career.
In some instances, parents may even need to consult professional
counselors for good insights.

12. *Love!* The unanimous advice of counselors, successful parents, and discerning teen-agers is this: "Let there never be any
question in the child's mind that, regardless of what the child
has been or has done, and regardless of what discipline requires
the parent to do, *the parent loves the child!*"

While it is not possible for parents to *like* everything a child
may do, it is both possible and imperatively important that nothing
be said during times of reproof and punishment to indicate that
the parent's love for the child is endangered. It is wholesome for
the erring child to know that his actions have impaired the *happiness* of the parent and even the child's attractiveness to the
parent temporarily. These impressions can be constructive factors. Yet, it is of vast importance that the child know that *all*
the things the parent does in teaching, insisting, reproof, and even
chastisement are a proof that the parent *cares* so greatly, and
that, just as the Heavenly Father chasteneth those whom he loves,
love impelling him to do so, the earthly parent acts thus because
he loves the child.

Other Voices

In concluding this chapter on discipline, I feel that it will be of interest and help to share several lists of suggestions which other writers have offered in this important matter.

I. William E. Homan's *Child Sense,* chapter 2, offers four suggestions:

1. Be an authority.
2. Be consistent.
3. Criticize the act, not belittling the person.
4. Avoid premature explanations.[9]

II. Siegfried and Therese Englemann in their book *Give Your Child a Superior Mind* (Simon and Schuster, 1964) suggest these guidelines:

1. Be consistent.
2. Don't lie (in answering children's questions).
3. Don't over-answer questions. There are times, particularly with little children, in which too much answering loses the point of the child's needing to obey because the parent has asked it.
4. Don't be afraid to show your ignorance (when children ask questions for which you do not have the answer at hand). This may afford an opportunity for a joint search for reasons.
5. Give the child plenty of free time—time in which he can work out in tangible ways some of the rules affecting his life.
6. Help your child to develop a positive (but realistic) image of himself.
7. Help the child to develop desirable personality characteristics.

III. Judge Leo B. Blessing, answering the oft-asked question, "But, Judge, What *Is* Proper Discipline?" gives ten suggestions;

1. Invite your child's confidences; don't demand them.
2. Avoid comparing your children.
3. Set a proper example for your children to follow.
4. Let parent groups help you establish reasonable guidelines for your children.

5. Try to see your child as others see him (not just his good points, but his weaknesses, too).
6. Don't be a buddy to your children—be a parent. ("Children need buddies, yes. But they need parents—to respect, admire, and emulate".)
7. (Parents should) Act together and consistently.
8. Apply discipline only to correct a child, not to punish him.
9. Let your child find his own level. ("Pressuring children to do more than they are capable of can make them hostile, defiant, frustrated, guilty, rebellious.")
10. Encourage your child to pursue his own ambitions. ("Parents who prod youngsters into unsuitable, unwanted careers may end up not with doctors and lawyers in the family, but with unemployable, unhappy adults who are frequently clients of doctors and lawyers." [10]

IV. The Christian Life Commission of the Baptist General Convention of Texas in its brochure, "Discipline in the Home," offers these eight "Guiding Principles For Discipline":

1. Love of the parents for the child is the most important ingredient in discipline.
2. Parents should agree regarding the disciplining of the children. . . . They should not differ over discipline in the presence of the child.
3. Parents should be consistent in discipline.
4. Parents should remember that discipline, to be effective, must begin early.
5. Parents should not punish the child to give expression to their own anger.
6. Parents should not hesitate to use physical punishment if and when it would be the most effective method of discipline. Spanking may clear the emotional air between a parent and child to the benefit of all concerned.
7. The parents should maintain regular family worship or devotions. There is a positive disciplinary value in the regular reading of God's Word and in prayer.
8. Parents should seek the leadership of the Lord in the training of their children, recognizing their responsibility to him for them.[11]

V. Dr. Clyde Narramore in his *Disciplining in the Christian Home,* extends his list of suggestions to twenty:

1. Let children know what is expected of them

2. Explain the reasons for rules
3. Make regulations flexible
4. Avoid unnecessary clashes of will.
5. Substitute acceptable activities (for those forbidden)
6. Teach children to be thoughtful of others.
7. Give children responsibility.
8. Avoid excessive criticism.
9. Teach your child to respect property rights.
10. Be a good listener.
11. Give children a part in family planning.
12. Share the family calendar.
13. Spend time with your child.
14. Assure your child that he is loved regardless of his misbehavior.
15. Look for causes of misbehavior.
16. Work toward self-discipline.
17. Consider your punishment.
18. Seek professional help (when needed)
19. Remember the impact of Christ-centered living upon discipline.
20. Pray for your child.[12]

In the spirit of Ecclesiastes ("Let us hear the conclusion of the whole matter"): the parent should strive to establish and maintain as fully as possible the ideal teacher-pupil relationship indicated by the word *discipline*—availing himself of the good counsel of both heaven and earth, exercising forever love, forgiveness, and patience, realizing that there are no perfect parents; and, having done his best for the child, to trust the child to come through to respectable adulthood.

To the parent who may feel bewildered and afraid in facing the very real and very large responsibility of disciplining children in a truly undisciplined age, the words of Dr. Homan may be comforting:

> To me, the perfect parent is simply the one who knows a good many of the right things to do in raising children, and who more than half the time does the right thing instead of the wrong. He is the parent who makes mistakes and then forgets them, and passes on to the next task with some thought to doing better.[13]

The counsel of Judge Blessing, mentioned above, concludes with this encouraging paragraph:

Happily, for the majority of youngsters, the prognosis is good. The difficult years will pass. If we can be patient with our children, be tolerant of their eccentricities, and—most important—enjoy them, they almost surely will make their way. If there is one thing which is likely to be a cure for adolescence, it's the passage of a few years.

And I suggest that the most helpful verse in the Bible for wondering parents is 1 Corinthians 13:4, "Charity (love) suffereth long, and is kind."

8

Communication and the Generation Gap

Some reader may be surprised by these two statements; 1. There has *always* been a generation gap between adults and young people; therefore, the much heralded "gap" is as "un-new" as the equally misnamed ancient immorality which sails under the misnomer of the "New Morality." 2. *There ought to be a gap!*

Concerning the antiquity of the generation gap, history, both sacred and secular, reveals that there has evidently been a difference of opinion, attitude, and preference between adults and their young through the centuries. Also, there have been many instances of youth rebellion through the centuries.

To mention but a few instances of the generation gap revealed in our Bible, let's begin with Cain, son of the first parents. As we recall, he rather blithely murdered his own brother out of envy; and when confronted by God, he replied flippantly, if not sarcastically, "Am I my brother's keeper?"

Samson, somewhat a precursor of the contemporary hippie, rejected vigorously the ideals and advice of his parents and practiced limitless sex, many other undisciplined desires, and a habit of destroying anything or anybody who sought to deter him. Does that remind you of what you've seen or read of some collegiate "doings" in recent years?

Eli's sons provide excellent early-day instances of children of active religionists in rebellion against parental hopes and ideals. (1 Sam. 2:22-3:14).

Jonathan, David's boon friend, was an early day instance of another version of the generation gap: his ideals were vastly superior to those of his father, King Saul—a kind of generation gap found frequently in our day!

Absalom must be another patron saint of present-day hippies —long hair and all—for, as we recall, he was evidently disappointed by the lapse between the ideals and actions of his father, David, whose sex partnership with another man's wife and the successful plan to dispose of the husband of his paramour may well have given to Absalom an alibi for his hostility. Absalom's active rebellion against his father, though working out in military action, reminds us of the tendency on the part of some of today's rebelling youth to be destructive when not granted their requests.

The books of Proverbs and Ecclesiastes are liberally punctuated by teachings which imply the ageless need for adults to give instruction, discipline, and example in dealing with youth; and they remind youth to listen to wisdom, lest the gap become an occasion for unfortunate conduct. Also, some passages in Paul's epistles seem to indicate that problems of the generation gap were present even early in the Christian era—Ephesians 6:1-4, for instance.

Secular history reveals, also, that in many eras there has been dismay on the part of adults by youth's disrespect of tradition and authority, its rebellious attitudes, and its tendency to destructiveness if denied its voice or freedom of action. There are recorded expressions of observers in ancient Athens and Rome to the effect that children were running wild, disobedient and disrespectful toward parents, law, and religion, and there are frequent predictions that young people "are going to the dogs." Evidences of "generation gaps" appear in drama and music of the centuries, also. Therefore, the "gap" has been with us always and is not new. The only new aspect of the gap is that young people of our day have been more vocal in pointing it out!

The Gap Is Normal

If, between the mature adulthood of parents and the lack of maturity on the part of inexperienced children—teen-agers, for instance—there is not a difference or "gap," either the parents have not matured, or the children are prodigious in their maturity! If parents have grown through the years, they will possess both knowledge of head and wisdom of experience not possible to their children.

What tragedy it is if parents do not have more enriched intelligence and seasoned judgment than their children twenty to thirty years younger! It is expecting the highly improbable, if not the impossible, that parents in their forties and their teen-agers should see and feel the same about issues concerning the teener's habits, dress, attitudes, associations.

It is very clear, therefore, that the gap cannot be and should not be *eliminated,* for that would be destructive to the balance of wholesome parent-child relationships; rather, the gap can be and should be *bridged.* With the gap bridged, it becomes entirely "passable" at every need of either parent or child for consultation, while maintaining a separateness of spheres necessary to mutual respect and wholesomeness.

Building the Bridge

Although the bridge needs to be built from both sides of the gap, it is largely the responsibility of the parents to plan, initiate, and develop the bridge; and, surprising as it may be to many parents, children in the great majority will welcome the bridge and cooperate in its construction and maintenance. Let's look now into some of the materials of which the bridge should be built.

1. *Respect.*—While respect of youngsters for parents is essential to the maintenance of happy parental authority, it needs to be a two-way respect. Children need parental respect for their hopes,

aspirations, desire for individual independence. They need respect for privacy in areas of life which are privacy-worthy, for their struggles to uphold their parents' ideals while seeking understandably the favor and approval of their peers. They need respect for their opinions—the willingness of parents to hear them out courteously and to give their opinions suitable consideration.

Repeatedly in my survey of teen-agers, there was the complaint that some parents seem to have no respect for the teener's opinions. If this feeling on the teen-ager's part is justified, he will come inevitably to the conclusion, "It doesn't matter to my parents what I think; they're going to have their way, regardless." If this situation persists, the bridge, even if constructed, will not be used by the teener.

Teeners replying to the questionnaire in my survey said many discerning things in this regard. Here are three samples:

> Parents should withhold judgment and punishment until their children have a fair chance to explain.
>
> I don't have any real serious problem with my parents. They are both Christians and have proved to be very understanding with all of my small problems. They usually let me say my part and explain my thoughts to them.
>
> If a young person has something or someone he cherishes quite a lot, don't cut it down; instead, reason it out if the parent has a good point.

2. *Remembering.*—"Parental amnesia" may not be epidemic in scope, but it is endemic in parentland, I glean from youth replies and articles by youth counselors; for so many parents seem to have forgot completely who and what they were in their teen years! This forgetting of their adolescent irritations, resentments, frustrations, feelings of being misunderstood, occasional loneliness, and incipient (though generally repressed) desire to rebel against parental control, and desire to "escape" to independence leaves parents unable to help their children cope with the same desires, desires made all the more turbulent today by overt rebellion on the part of so many young people.

I chuckled out loud in reading this remark by a teen-ager who participated in the survey: "You grownups were teen-agers once, too, and you won't ever catch me in a raccoon coat or swallowing goldfish." And he might have added, had he desired, "rolling bedsteads to the next town, packing telephone booths, or sitting on flagpoles for marathon periods"!

Remembering what we were and how we felt will make possible a fellow-feeling called *sympathy,* a rapport in which we know how the teen-ager feels, because we remember keenly our similar impulses in teen years. Mark Twain evidently kept remembering his adolescent feelings of superiority to parental judgment as indicated in this immortal observation: "When I was a boy of fourteen, my father was so ignorant I could hardly stand to have the old man around. But when I got to be twenty-one, I was astonished at how much the old man had learned in seven years."

Heaven help us to remember that we were not paragons of sweet understanding, reliability, and cooperation with parents when we were teen-agers!

3. *Understanding.*—There are many circumstances of our day as it impinges upon our teen-agers which are so different from those of our teen years, that a fellow-feeling (sympathy) is not possible. In these instances, however, using our lively imaginations, we can come to an objective understanding of the very subjective pressures with which our current young people are faced.

Here are some of the personal reminders given in my survey of teen-agers:

Parents need to realize that things are different (for teen-agers) from thirty years ago.

Remember they (today's teen-agers) and their time are not like it was when you were a teen. Things are different!

I think, foremost, you should include in your book a section to let parents know things have changed. They're different now, and we have to face situations with newer slants on life than our parents did. I'm sure parents are aware of the change, but still revert to old ways of thinking.

Understanding is not synonomous with *agreeing.* Understanding means that we do take cognizance that the circumstances under which our children grow up today *are* vastly different and more difficult than were the circumstances of our teen years. For most of us adults, our teen years found home, school, and church in a solid phalanx of character inculcation; society condemned and punished people for dishonesty and immorality; parents in a community were generally of strength to each other in maintaining the same standards and rules. Situation Ethics, the New(?) Morality, and the "God Is Dead" clique had not "dawned" upon our world to "release" us from the bondage of antiquity!

What an almost total difference today imposes upon our young people! Therefore, they need and deserve fuller explanations of ideals, a compassionate sharing of reasons, a patient reemphasis when peers press upon them, an inculcation of courage beyond anything most parents ever needed in their teen years, and a patience from parents as they (teeners) try to handle the pressures without losing favor or friends.

4. *Standing.*—While exercising sympathy and understanding toward today's young people, parents need more than ever to *stand by* the values without which strong character cannot develop. Copious testimonies from young people and their counselors attest to the wisdom of the parents' standing firmly for important principles of character and behavior. Some delightful replies to my questionnaire are in point:

Children think much more highly of parents when they stick with their rulings instead of giving in. Children do appreciate these parents *very, very, very* much, although it may not show.

Parents, please do not let us run wild, regardless of how much we appear to resent your strictness. Something "way down deep inside us" tells us you are right, but we are afraid that the crowd will call us "square" if we don't run with it. If you would just say no and make it stick, you would often give us protection which we need from the pressures of the crowd.

Stanley Jacobs, in his article, "How to Talk to a Teen-Ager ... Maybe!" offers this pertinent counsel to parents:

> Don't be eager to agree to everything a youngster says, in order to be a good guy. If he says something outrageous or wrong to which you react strongly, speak up! You may fear that he thinks your view of life is "square." But if this is the way you feel, *say so*. Youngsters joke about "squares," but they respect conviction and forthrightness. On the other hand, affably agreeing with every faddish or shallow view voiced by young people—in order to make them accept you—merely convinces them that you are superficial and afraid of arguing with them.[1]

If parents do not stand by right principles of conduct, their youngsters will not need to cross the bridge to the parents' side of the gap. They will know without asking that the parent will "give in."

5. *Listening.*—If youngsters know that, while their parents will stand by tested principles, they will hear the child all through, permitting him to state his case and reasons fully, being willing to engage in an honest dialogue, that is a great comfort to the child and the basis for both admiration and love. Because many situations in contemporary society are not as clear in the classification of "right" or "wrong" to the teen-ager's mind as they are to the adult mind, parents need to know clearly what the teener is thinking, in order to be helpful in bringing the situation under discussion into a perspective which is reasonable to the young person's mind.

Genuine *listening* will help parents to discern more accurately the child's thought patterns, convictions, strengths, and weaknesses and will assist the parent to a fuller understanding of the pressures under which the child lives. Intelligent listening, without necessarily agreeing, can give any parent a teen-ager's view of any city's social life and problems, including some information on adult shortcomings which the parent may have missed hearing at coffee break! Teeners "know the score" on adults in any town! Parents need to be *available* for listening (not probing) at the times in which their youngsters are most likely to need to talk: in coming in from school, in getting back from athletic contests and other school events in which they participated or in which they were enthusiastically interested, in getting back from dates and social events, in returning from camps or other trips, and following meaningful religious services in which the youngsters have been involved. When young people need to talk to their parents, they want to talk *right then.* As one teen-ager in the survey observed, "Guide a teen-ager when you notice something is bothering him. Don't have something else to do, for someday you may be sorry."

6. *Learning.*—In keeping the generation gap bridged through respecting, remembering, understanding, standing, and listening, the parent will experience a learning process—learning techniques which "get through" more reasonably to the youngsters, sensitive areas which need a deft approach, when to talk and when not to talk, how much explanation and "reasons" the child needs, and when to terminate discussions.

Some parents seem never to learn, because they do not really listen. Stanley Jacobs' article, cited above, related the experiences of two teen-agers:

My parents don't accept my feelings as *real!* If I'm moody, they try to order me out of my blues, or they attempt bribery, such as a new dress; or they poke fun at me for being a spoilsport in the family. Neither Mom nor Dad ever takes time to sit down and find out what really bugs me. It's as if they are afraid of serious conversation with their own daughter.

My dad thinks that giving advice is a substitute for conversation. Oh, he'll give me orders and suggestions without end, but if I want to find out what he really thinks about something—whether it's dating, cheating on my exams, politics, or religion—he clams up. Talk with my dad is a one-way street, *his way.*[2]

In both of the foregoing instances, both the teen-ager and the parent lost so much of the opportunity to learn—the teen-ager from the parent, and the parent from the teen-ager—because parents did not listen.

Another learning dividend from listening is this: an adult cannot actually understand the feelings, reactions, hopes, fears, desires, and the basic (though often well disguised) compassions of young people without listening respectfully and searchingly to them. By intelligent listening the adult may well come to a discovery of dimensions of goodness and strength in today's "strange" teen-agers which will amaze him.

I have learned from listening—not to the shouters, disrupters, and four-letter-word specialists, but to many of our finest and most serious youngsters—that their apparent restlessness with the adult status-defenders grows out of their being more compassionately interested in righting wrongs, correcting inequities, and making more *real* in daily life the teachings of Christ and the principles of democracy than any youth group in our nation's history. And the young people to whom I have listened and from whom I have learned are willing and eager to be "up and gone" to the task of making Christianity and democracy more meaningful!

Do you know why some of our finest young people like certain types of contemporary music which send the traditionalists into near shock? I listened to their reasons and learned! They like it because of its freedom from the forms and restrictions of the more formal music—its very freedom from "the establishment" appeals to them. They like it because it is fresh, spontaneous, and often appealing to their moods of loneliness. They like it because it is typically the creation of youth, and because of its democracy: anybody can "get in on it" without prior musical knowledge or advantage. They like it because it transcends all barriers of race, culture, and nationality, and seems to "make of one" all youth of the world—an ideal which not many of their parents have yet embraced! They like it because some of it speaks of peace, which the devotees of Aquarius are not alone in desiring!

(Let me confess that my preferences are *still* on the side of the more nearly traditional music, but I wouldn't raise a finger to rob today's young people of the music they prefer. I have listened to their reasons, and I understand why they like this particular type of contemporary music. I am bearing up bravely, sustained by this assurance: I have seen enough youth generations move into adulthood to know that today's devotees to the rock beat will be tomorrow's devotees to a music type more fully identified with their adult roles. Meanwhile, may Heaven help us all to survive the deafening decibels of today's resounding music with enough hearing to permit us to enjoy once again Tchaikovsky's Fifth!)

7. *Admitting.*—If parents are willing to admit their lack of information or insight in some discussions with their growing youngsters, suggesting that "we look together for the answers," the admission can make the parent-child rapport a mutual search for knowledge and can remove the false halo of "I know it all: don't disagree with me" which some teen-agers see about their parents' heads!

Admitting, too, to being in error if, upon fuller information parents find that they were wrong in a judgment or accusation, prevents the possible feeling and sarcastic expression on the part of the teener of "Aw, of *course,* you're right and I'm wrong. It's *always* that way. So, pardon me for being alive!"

One of the warmest expressions of admiration for parents found in my survey of teen-agers indicated a complete willingness on the part of parents of a teen-age boy to talk things through unhurriedly, giving the teen-ager full and fair opportunity to disclose his point of view; and the teener's report concluded with these significant words: "And if they find they were wrong, they apologize."

Although it is beyond question that parents who are committed to the highest ideals of character will be in error much less frequently than will their offspring, it is highly possible for our finite, non-omniscient judgment to make an occasional mistake; and it will be a wholesome exercise in humility to admit the mistake. Remember Dr. Louis Evans' magnificent observation: "The six bravest, hardest words in the English language are, 'I was wrong; I am sorry.'"

8. *Trusting.*—In the full awareness of youth's limitations in conviction and, possibly, in courage, parents will be wise to begin trusting their children as early as the children are able to understand fully parental expectations of them. If the trust is betrayed, the experience becomes an excellent opportunity for teaching that privileges are withdrawn for reasons which the child cannot dispute. If the trust is honored, the honoring becomes the basis for fuller trust in the future—with the young person understanding *why.* For the great majority of young people, the awareness of being trusted by their parents is a powerful inducement to obedience when out of the parents' sight.

9. *Waiting.*—Patience is a virtue not found widely in today's youth constituency, but it surely needs to be in the "armory" of parents in their dealing with children who are growing up! The tendency to "explode" over even minor differences or infractions may well destroy a section or the whole of the bridge over the generation gap, with the result that the explosion-prone parent may well not be approached by the teener except in the direst need.

Patience will sustain the parent in teaching, reemphasizing, illustrating, and trying again in instances of slow perception or stubbornness on the part of the child. Patience will help the parent to help the erring child to "start all over again" with encouragement to do better next time. Patience will keep the parent from giving up hope for the apparently incorrigible teen-ager and, surely, from ever telling that teener, "You're simply hopeless; you'll land in the penitentiary, for sure; I've just given up hope on you!"

Some parents who read these lines can attest that some young-sters in their families who once seemed to be headed for the penitentiary are now in pulpits and other positions of tremendous blessing to society—and one of the factors in their being where they are now is the patience of their parents.

Doing or having done everything they can do to guide a young-ster toward wholesome living, wise parents will *wait* before writing the final verdict; and, while waiting, they will hope and pray and believe that the seeds they have planted *will* eventually germinate and grow up into fruitful lives. The glorious assurance of thous-ands of parent-teams who waited is that the waiting has been more than compensated in the joyous gratitude which their once-bitter teen-agers now shower upon them.

10. *Easing-Salving.*—When the blow of correction, reproof, or ultimatum must fall (and fall it must in many instances), parents can soften the humiliation of the blow and the wound of the hurt in giving the "come uppance" as *tactfully* as possible and wise.

Shouting, screaming, and humiliating a youngster in the presence of others is rarely, if ever, wise procedure. I admit that there may well be a few teen-agers for whom *only* the shouting-screaming-humiliating technique will get results sufficient to keep him out of prison; yet, the number of such armadillo-type characters is not large. For the overwhelming majority of teen-agers—far more sensitive than their casual manner indicates—a firm, low-decibel, pleasant-as-possible technique is more resultful in the long run.

Two teen-ager replies in the survey are enlightening:

Don't make a mountain out of a mole hill when we make some small mistake. Smile at us, remind us of what we did wrong, and we'll try extra hard to please them next time. . . . I do agree to occasional strict discipline, but nothing harsh or cruel.

Tell parents not to force us into such a corner in times of discussion and reproof that there's no way out for us except a humiliating way. . . . If they would just leave some way in which we could 'admit' our way out without being crushed, our consciences would do the humiliating, and the thoughtfulness of our parents in giving us a chance to 'work our way out' would increase our affection for them.

11. *Laughing.*—A sense of humor in parent-child relationships can reduce voltage in situations which, without humor, could be likely to create major tension and, perhaps, unnecessary eruptions of hostility. There are times in which laughing at small mistakes is reproof enough; for, though almost everybody enjoys being laughed *with*, nobody really enjoys being laughed *at*.

In my years as a disciplinarian in a college situation, I fell upon this thought in the midst of being almost distracted by mounting instances in which student actions "riled" me: Why not separate the actions which irritate you into two divisions—those which, though they are irritative, are not a violation of moral principle, and (2) those which do involve moral principle; stop worrying about the first group and save your energies and disposition for handling the second group?

Once the division was made, I felt relaxed and was then in position to see some humor in the actions which, though irritative, violated neither moral principle nor college rules. Another decade of living in the midst of the same circumstances left me "unscarred," with a multitude of student friends, and with a sense of humor which has helped me in hundreds of high school groups to handle difficult discussions and questions forcefully, but with a "certain touch" which has brought agreement in delighted laughter from students instead of scowling disagreement.

A sense of humor in dealing with children in the family situation leaves happy memories about little matters instead of wounds from memories of "too much ado about practically nothing." Laughter can, indeed, lubricate the communication pattern in a family as lubricants help machinery to run more smoothly; and, to continue the comparison, the lubricating sense of humor will prevent unnecessary "burnings of bearings" and breakdowns in continuing good rapport within the family.

12. *Loving.*—Although "liking" may have its ups and downs and may well vacillate according to moods and actions, *loving* should never be a questionable factor in parent-child relations. In day-by-day relationships, in times of frank and tense discussion of attitudes and actions, and in times of punishment it is of tremendous importance that the child know that the parental attitude or action is a very real dimension and proof of love.

In a recent editorial of one of our daily papers, there was this highly relevant suggestion:

A woman with long experience in dealing with runaway girls in a large city found the one thing that stood out as a cause was the lack of affection in the home. She declared: "I have not had a single girl among the runaways who had experienced normal affection in her home while she was growing up."

You may easily take affection in the home for granted, particularly if you are busy at work or a ceaseless round of activities outside the home. Whatever the cause, if you are tired or weighted down with duties, problems, or demands upon your time on the outside, it may be difficult to prove your affection to members of your family.

When emotional needs go unsatisfied, happiness suffers from poor nourishment. Everyone needs affection. There is no adequate substitute for affection, regardless of age.[3]

One of the strangest developments of our times is this startling fact, revealed unmistakably in surveys, conferences, and testimonies: A much higher number of love-starved youngsters come from homes with excellent financial and social ratings—families in which, distressingly often, parents have tried to substitute material things, often extravagantly expensive, for genuine love—than from homes of lesser status, but with the priceless gift of wholesome love for the children.

The most eloquent observation given in this regard in the teenagers' replies to my survey was given by an almost twenty-year-old boy: "Although there were many times in which I felt that my parents did not understand me, and even times in which I felt that they were unreasonable, I never for a moment doubted that they loved me very much. I want to be the kind of parent my parents have been, so that my children someday will be able to say: " 'Dad was as strict as the Ten Commandments; but, we always knew for sure that he loved us!' "

Some Concluding Reminders

1. Developing the gap-bridging traits listed and discussed above may be easier for some parents than for others; yet, an honest and continuing effort to develop and master those traits is a *must* for parents who want to keep the firmest and happiest bridge across the gap.

2. Excellent and satisfying communication is not a *continuum* (that is, a continuing matter without interruptions), even with the most approachable child in the family. There will be times in which it is both easy and joyous to communicate; there will be other times in which the parents will feel that their words are falling on unhearing ears, or that the ears are not in a mood to listen. Wise parents will sense the highly receptive signals which the youngster gives and will capitalize upon those times and will, furthermore, not be dismayed at the times of nonreceptivity.

3. As parents of several children know, doubtless, no two children in the same family will have the same receptivity to communication, and the same techniques or combination of techniques will not necessarily "work" with every child. The parent who genuinely desires to communicate with children will, therefore, search diligently and patiently for the formula of communication which bridges the gap for each child.

But of this we can be sure: parents who love their children enough, who develop the factors which make for good communication, who study their individual children earnestly to discern the most successful approaches, who try diligently . . . and try again, who don't despair of bridging the gap will eventually do so. It may be no more than a look in the child's eyes, or a quiet smile of warmth, or a nod of the head, or a "gotcha, Mom" reply, but you will know that you "got through" to the youngster's side of the gap.

Or if you don't discern it immediately, that youngster in his twenties or thirties will fill the hunger of your heart with such words as "Mom and Dad, you may have thought I wasn't listening or caring back then, but you were getting through to me better than you thought!"

9

Because You Asked

(Answers to Specific Questions)

On the questionnaires returned by the parent teams in my survey, there were specific requests for answers to parent-teen problems. The twelve most frequently asked questions are shared here with my replies—many of which are replies based on interviews with parents.

1. *Is there a recommended beginning age for dating and for steady dating?*

A survey of teen-age counselors throughout America produced this suggested schedule for dating:

Ages 13 and 14: no "single dating" or "full-fledged dating" because of a lack of personality-wide maturity; but, because of the desirability of developing social association and acceptability, "group dating" may be permitted. As you would surmise, this implies that several boys and girls would be together for specific times of social activity.

Age 15: Although some group dating would continue, *occasional* single dating may be permitted—as the occasions justify, but not necessarily a date every week.

Age 16: Regular dating—at regularly agreed upon times weekly. Although the "with whom?" and "where?" items will need to be discussed by parent and teen-ager, the "when?" aspect will have been settled on a rather permanent basis. *Steady dating,* according to the unanimous judgment of the adult counselors who had worked with teen-agers, had best not begin before 17.

2. *What shall I tell my teen-ager who says, "But I can't be popular if I don't do what my crowd is doing"?*

These approaches are worth trying:

(1) Try to sell your teen-ager on the fact that popularity comes
in two brands: *temporary* and *permanent,* or *instant* and *eternal.*
You may illustrate by contrasting cheap but "catchy" music with
the music of the great masters. The average "popular" song blazes
like a meteor across the horizon, and everybody seems to go for
it; yet, in most of those songs, the music and words are not
really good music and not good literature. Therefore, in a matter
of months that number is gone and forgotten. On the other hand,
the music whose words and melody are based upon the highest
ideals of literature and musicology will live through the centuries
—not as popular at first, but increasingly admired as time proceeds.

So with art. The pictures which appeal only to the shallow
instincts or fads of the time may have crowds singing their praises
today, while the pictures which are painted upon the principles
of art which endure may not draw the crowds immediately. Let
time pass, however, and the cheaper pictures are discarded and
forgotten, while the true art of the great pictures keeps them alive
through the centuries in ever-increasing worth. Rembrandt's group
portrait, "The Night Watch," was so little appreciated immediately
that the artist received only 150 guilders for it. More recently the
curators of the museum in which the picture hangs were offered
several million dollars for it.

(2) The individual who declines to compromise will not be
unpopular if he declines or dissents *gracefully.* It is usually the
individual who is waspy or condemnatory of others or the "holier-
than-thou" attitude which will diminish the popularity of an individual who sticks by his convictions.

(3) Despite the apparent concurrence of some young people
with the wrong which the gang may agree to do, there is a basic
decency in the hearts of most of them—a decency which will cause
them to admire your courage—that is, if it is a radiant contagious

courage. Some of them will tell you some day, even if privately, of their admiration, and eventually some of them will join you.

(4) Would you prefer that they praise you openly for compromising your principles, cheapening yourself in the compromise, or that they admire you privately for your character and courage? Would you prefer to be popular for a little time now or increasingly high in the esteem of your buddies as they mature in their ideals? Honestly now, would you choose to be a "flash in the pan" for a short time and then forgotten—or to be seen retrospectively as an admirable guy or girl and remembered forever as an inspiration?

(Note to parents: Don't be surprised if, after you have shared the foregoing information, your teener gives you a withering look and an ego-crushing blow with "Aw, Mom . . . Dad, how corny can you be?" Don't despair, parent: that's not the final evaluation your teener will give. Patience and faith will help you to await the verdict of your teen-ager's mature years: "Mom . . . Dad, you were *so* right!")

3. *I am aghast at the poor attitudes and poor sense of values of my teen-ager. What can I do to improve them?*

Parents will do well to remember that the society in which today's teen-agers live is like no other before it, and that our youngsters are surrounded, bombarded, and pressured by attitudes and values foreign to most of us adults. So, it is not so much a rebellion against parents—this strange set of attitudes and values—as it is a reflection of the teen society in which they are immersed daily.

Remember, too, that, though your teen-age attitudes and values were not as different from those of your parents as are those of your children from yours, you probably didn't have your present mature commitment to values when you were a teener. Therefore, you can be reasonably sure that some of your teener's present attitudes and values will pass with the coming of maturity. I have seen so many "impossible" teen-agers develop into incredibly fine, stable, inspiring twenty- and thirty-year oldsters!

Remember, also, that much of the teener's apparent attitudes may well be only surface conformity to his peers, and that deep within himself he *knows* that the better ways you are pointing out *are* better. That may well be why he appears to be irked when you remind him of the better values. He thinks that you are smart enough to know that he really knows better, and that you should have understood that his surface didn't really reflect his soul!

What To Do

a. Expose the youngster's mind and heart to as many good influences as possible outside the home:

(1) Encourage and support church and school seminars, lectures, and the like which bring persons of high ideals and values into contact with the youth group of which your teener is a part. Some adult leaders of youth have remarkably good rapport with teen-agers; and, since they are not emotionally involved, as are parents, they can get across effectively many of the values which parents want their youngsters to accept.

(2) Send the youngster to as many good youth retreats, summer camps, and similar activities as possible. High ideals are a vital part of both program and leadership in these youth gatherings.

(3) Even if the size of your church and its budget do not permit a full-time director of youth activity, try with other parents, even at sacrifice, to arrange for a weekend or summer employment of an attractive, well-balanced, youth-oriented college or seminary student to come to your church to work with youth.

b. Provide wholesome books and periodical materials of good youth appeal for your home—but no nagging of the teen-ager to read them, please! Just make sure that the books and magazines are there within sight and reach, and depend upon normal curiosity to lead the teen-ager to explore the material. Don't necessarily expect him or her to tell you that the reading helped. You can be reasonably sure, however, that the reading planted seeds of thought which will bear fruit later.

c. In discussions of attitudes and values, try hard to persuade your teen-ager to take the long look to discern what values will best stand the test of the years, and which values will bring more of happiness. Pointing out adults in whose lives one can see the fruition of the best values will be helpful, particularly if your teener admires the adults pointed out.

d. *Wait* prayerfully, hopefully, patiently, taking care not to destroy the communication bridge between yourself and the teen-ager, regardless of the irritation!

4. *How can we impress upon our children the importance of avoiding vulgar speech and obscene literature?*

It isn't easy—what with a proliferation of four-letter words in practically every medium which reaches the ear and eye, and with the shockingly loose speech of so many adults in high and honorable positions—not to mention their high school associations! But it *is* important to try your best to guide your youngsters to absolute decency in speech and reading.

Is it necessary to mention again that good parental example is of paramount importance? Parents, who only occasionally drop a risque word, need not be surprised that a child, whose alert ears were listening—perhaps, for an alibi for his own loose speech—may come through with his own version of the risque. More than that, parents whose exclamations are slang-filled are saying rather clearly that good taste in speech isn't important. So, the parents whose conversations are dotted with "Heck," "Gosh," "Golly," "Darn," and "I didn't do a blame thing," should not drop their dentures if their youngsters use the originals of which the aforementioned words are pronouns!

If the parents' speech habits have a clean bill of health, they are in position to do several things:

a. To place great importance upon the use of completely clean speech.

b. To insist upon good taste in speech—with reproofs, even penalties for a youngster's dropping below the level of decency in speech.

c. To encourage (even with rewards) the building of good vocabularies with emphasis upon descriptives, exclamatories, synonyms, and the like.

d. To insist upon a youngster's dropping regular associations with peers who have dirty speech.

In the matter of *reading materials,* parents have a heavy responsibility to condemn the wrong and to provide the right kinds of reading. In the condemnation, it will be useful to help youngsters to realize that "As he (a man) thinketh in his heart, so is he" (Prov. 23:7) is a vital truth—that it is impossible to read filth without its leaving an imprint in the mind, and that, since the thought is "father to the act," the filth-reader submits himself to the possibility of acting as he has read. And parents surely have the right and responsibility to work with other adults to reduce or eliminate the sources of obscene literature sold in the community.

Condemnation is not enough, however. The responsibility to introduce children to good reading and to provide such reading for them is clear. Once I knew parents who surrounded their two young sons with excellent music from their infancy forward. As the boys grew to the level of understanding music, the parents interpreted the musical selections and thereby the boys developed understanding and appreciation of truly good music. As the boys grew into their high school and college years, they heard much of the music of popular youth appeal; and, though they didn't "see red" at hearing music of temporary worth and appeal, they had such good grounding in really good music, that they were never really "taken in" by the cheaper music. Isn't it possible that a similar situation could develop with an early introduction to and continuing association with good reading?

Remember, too, if you have given adequate sex instruction, if you have provided the finest materials for reading in sex development, and if the communication gap has been kept open, the appeal of filthy materials on sex will have much less attraction—if, indeed, any at all—to your children than to the children whose parents gave them no opportunity to know the truly happy and beautiful information concerning the purpose of sex.

5. *What is a good approach in counseling a teen-ager concerning the dangers of necking and petting?*

If the quality and quantity of sex instruction, including wholesome reading, have been clear and adequate, it will be easy to show the relationship between promiscuous handling of each other's bodies and premarital sex. If the importance of waiting for marriage in this important relationship has been convincing, the danger which excited and inflamed bodies pose will be evident. Statistics concerning premarital pregnancies of high school girls are published periodically, and these reports speak their own eloquent but tragic message concerning the ultimate result of necking and petting.

Some columnists who write with teen-agers in mind offer pamphlets on necking and petting. There are some helpful titles in our resource-book list at the conclusion of this volume. Also, on pages 47 and 48 of *The Teen-Age Slant* (Broadman Press, Nashville) there is a terse, but adequate discussion which parents may well place in the hands of their youngsters to acquaint them with the principles involved in necking and petting.

6. *We have been distressed by the recent indications that many young people do not respect law and order. How can we instil that respect in our children?*

The home with its rules, "superior officers" (parents), and individuals who are taught to take the rights of others into consideration is an excellent laboratory for preparing youngsters for their later needs in school and society to respect law, order, and the rights of others. The importance of obedience to family regulations—with penalties for disobedience, the necessity of respect for parents, and the insistent obligation to respect the rights of others will help to establish the youngster's patterns of relationship to the larger involvement in society.

Parental example again! Parents who violate traffic regulations, who are not averse to fudging in relationships in business or in tax paying, and who laugh at "clever" ways of evading law, or who are forever criticizing the laws should not expect their looking, listening children to be paragons of respect for the law.

Also, parents may well instigate and support school and church panels, seminars, and lectures which encourage young people to respect law and the rights of others.

7. *How can we deepen the concern of our children for God, the Bible, prayer, and the church?*

All of us are aware that most children pass through phases in their relationship to church and religious practices—often from deep devotion and high enthusiasm to lessening interest, to outright indifference, to evident hostility, to rebellion in the matters of attendance, participation, and cooperation, later to return to devotion and commitment. Some of the reasons for the phases are understandable: the normal truculence of adolescent years, the desire to "cut the apron strings," the growing desire for independence of thought and action with the attendant feeling that devotion to church is "kid stuff," and the example of many of their teen friends whose parents have let them drop out of church.

In some instances, the teen-ager is trying to establish his own value system and is detaching himself from the church to get an objective and comparative view of its values. In some instances, the teen-ager just doesn't know *why* he wants to drop out of church and to drop former religious habits and practices.

What to Do

In the home, the family can maintain an attractive daily devotional period, using the newer translations of the Bible, employing the new devotional cassette tapes, varying even with filmstrips, slides, and other types of equipment which make the Bible truths attractive and practical. Also, attractive youth oriented publications can be kept within reach of the children. Above all, parents will try valiantly to *live* the radiant truths of Christianity in the home, in their inter-personal relationships, and in work-time relationships. Love, forgiveness, and patience will often prevent a break between parents and children in the matters of church life and religious practices generally.

If youth leadership or youth direction in the church is not attractive and relevant, and if youth activities do not include the compassionate outreach to permit young people to help disadvantaged people in the community, do your best in consultations with pastor and church leaders to bring the church youth programs to a state of genuine youth appeal and challenge.

Encourage your lethargic teen-ager to attend youth retreats and camps in which both leadership and youth associations may give your son or daughter a new concept of the significance of church and religious life and new motivation for participation.

Don't give up and don't close the communication bridge through impatience! Tomorrow or next week or next year, you may discover that your tantalizing teen-ager has made a full circle and is even more genuinely committed to God, the Bible, prayer, and the church than ever before.

8. *How shall we handle the problem of irresponsibility on the part of our children?*

The parents with whom I have discussed this problem agree that their most successful technique has been to relate *privilege* to *responsibility:*

a. In conduct, including respect for parents, obedience to family rules, and regard for the rights of other family members.

b. In the performance of regular or assigned duties as a member of the family.

Responsibility brings privileges; irresponsibility forfeits privileges.

Several parents reported that summer camp sessions for their children had improved obedience, cooperation, and even courtesy. Several parents suggested that "hard cases" of irresponsibility on the part of boys had been "cured" by sending sons to good preparatory military schools.

I am inclined to believe that, in almost all instances, the relating of privilege to responsible behavior and performance of home tasks will suffice to bring desired results.

9. *How early in child-rearing should parents begin to urge self-discipline?*

Parents who were interviewed have offered these suggestions:

a. That children, varying in the rate of growth and maturity, logically vary in ages at which self-discipline can have its beginning.

b. That self-discipline can begin earlier in most children than parents think.

c. That self-discipline in all aspects of a child's life cannot be achieved simultaneously, that the spontaneity and exuberance of childhood and the growing-up years could be inhibited if a too-comprehensive attempt at inculcating self-discipline is undertaken simultaneously.

Interviewed parents suggested that, beginning with the self-discipline of toilet habits, the encouragement to self-discipline may well move on to food and eating habits, sleep and bedtime patterns, temper tantrums, playtime habits, sibling relationships; and, as the child enters school and proceeds through the at-home years, the self-discipline encouragement will include all the factors which make for health, attractiveness of appearance, good character traits, wholesome interpersonal relationships, academic achievement, and spiritual growth.

10. *Our teen-ager is the personification of apathy. How can we help to motivate him?*

"I'd like to put a firecracker under him to get him moving," one distraught father told me in discussing his apathetic son. A mother speaking of her daughter, said, "She's just not interested in *anything!*" So, parent reader, if you have a lethargic teen-ager, your misery has right much company! *Is there anything you can do?* These suggestions may not turn the trick with your teen-ager, but other parents have tried one or more of them with some success:

    a. Talk with school counselors and teachers to ascertain their judgment concerning your teener. If from them you can discern what things seem to appeal most to your teen-ager (academically and in student activity), what they feel his problem or problems may be, what suggestions they have to offer for joint home-school cooperation, you may derive some ideas for motivation.

    b. If your church has a director of youth activities, make inquiries of that source, also. An objective view can often spot tensions, conflicts, and bright spots which the more subjective view of parents may not see.

    c. If there is an older young person or even an adult for whom your teener has admiration, you may wish to ask such a person to help you find the key to "sparking" your teen-ager into more initiative and creativity.

    d. If you or others can help the teen-ager make a challenging vocational choice, you may be able to show him or her the importance of "getting with it" academically and in total personality improvement in order to make sure of getting into the preferred college and of being accepted as a responsible prospect for the vocation chosen.

    e. Again, some parents have recommended a good summer camp as providing associations, atmosphere, and counseling which can help in dispelling apathy.

    f. Though it may puncture your parental ego and leave you with the feeling, "Well, of all things . . . ," here's a possibility: what your wisdom, teaching, insisting, and even threatening may not have accomplished, a romantic interest in a splendid member of the opposite sex may well accomplish! Her blue eyes, her blonde or brunette tresses, and her trusting of that hunk of teen-age masculinity whom you call "Son" just could work wonders with your son . . . or with your daughter with the situation reversed. So, if the object of his or her affection is a truly fine person, don't panic. Your prayer for a lazy son or lethargic daughter may be answered in a manner you had not dreamed!

11. *How far should parents go in "laying down the law" in such matters as hair, clothes, and the like?*

At the cost of being facetious, I am offering this observation: Never before have parents and children "got in each other's hair" as thoroughly about any differences as in the contemporary difference over hair length, hair condition, and clothes! While some teen-age boys point out to their parents that men in biblical times wore long hair and beards and prophesied, parents point out a much more contemporary impression of male long hair addicts— hippies, drug users, and sex libertines.

What shall parents do in regard to what they regard as "outlandish" modes of hair style and dress? Again I have been obliged to rely upon parents of contemporary teen-agers for suggestions, some of which are these:

a. Some parents have adopted the "shape up or ship out" rule: "You either get that hair cut and your dress made acceptable, or you leave home!"

b. Other parents have set limits, agreeing to a reasonable length of a son's hair and a degree of conformity in dress for son and daughter—but definitely understood limits.

c. Still other parents have done nothing and have simply endured the present mod styles of hair and dress.

d. A variation of suggestion number *b* (above) is followed by some parents: The parent and teen-ager "negotiate," with

the teener agreeing to the limitations, and with the parents'
reciprocating by making concessions or privileges in other
ways which do not compromise principle.

Would you be willing to have an observation from a nonparent? Although I am not a parent, I am a constant confidant of
teen-agers. In the light of many and continuing years of asso-
ciating, observing, and counseling with them, here is my observation: *If my teen-agar would promise me upon his honor to abstain
from liquor and drugs, to wait for marriage in the matter of sex,
and to be honest in word and deed, I could "stand" some aberra-
tions from the norm in hair and dress.*

Quite naturally, I would definitely prefer his adhering more
closely to accepted standards of dress and hair; yet, honesty,
decency, and discipline in character are vastly more important
to his future than how his exterior looks during the teen years. I
have seen teeners immaculately garbed and groomed, but who
were careless in the more important matters mentioned above. I've
seen some teen-agers, too, whose hair was longer and who would
never have made the fashion magazines in dress, but who were
tender of heart and truly clean in habits. Of course, the teener
can have *both*—acceptable appearance and sterling character; yet,
if the choice must be made, this nonparent who knows personally
so many of your teeners would choose the character strength,
rejoicing in the assurance that these, too (hair style and dress),
will pass away!

12. *Do any parents ever work out an amicable arrangement for
the use of the telephone and family car by teen-agers?*

Whoever comes up with a universally acceptable and appli-
cable answer to that question will deserve a Congressional Medal,
a Nobel Peace Prize, and a lifetime annuity! My inquiries reveal
that some families have worked out plans which are acceptable
to those particular families, but not acceptable to other families.

The Car Problem

If your family belongs to the economic stratum of *plenty plus,* you can solve the problem of conflicting schedule claims on car use by providing a car for each family member who is old enough to have a driver's license. This suggestion will not solve the problem in the great majority of families and, most surely, not for the family which has only one car; nor will the car-for-every-member solve the problem of traffic violations, accidents, coming-in hours, and the like.

In families in which one or more old-enough-to-drive teen-agers are involved and individual cars are not available, some have had these guidelines:

a. The family compares and discusses schedules of activity at the outset of each week, particularly evening and night-time uses apart from regularly scheduled work-time or regular family uses, listing individual desires for use of the car. If two wishes conflict in time, priority is discussed. The priority factors are these: comparative importance of the two needs involved, priority of time in which request for use of car was made, and the possibility of adjusting the hours of use, so that both of the competing parties can have use of the car.

b. If the competitors for use of the car are both teen-agers, parents discuss the possibility of simultaneous use of the car —as in double dating, or in one teen-ager's taking the other to his appointment first, picking him up later, and reversing the arrangement in a later time of conflict.

c. Even if there is no conflict in times in which the car is needed, some parents relate the use of the car to the teen-agers' cooperation, obedience, and dependability in the use of the car.

None of these plans will work all the time in your family? Join the club of a large number of parents who are looking for the perfect formula! This problem, like the poor, "ye have always with you"!

The Telephone

Although the financial problem in providing individual cars for teen-agers is impossible in most families—and even in some instances actually unwise, the possibility of a separate telephone (not an extension!) for teen-agers may be both possible and wise. In the separate telephone arrangement, two or more teen-agers can work out their own conflicts in times and conversation length with whatever parental mediation the case may require. Also, the use of the parents' telephone is off-limits except by parental permission and with a parent-fixed time limit for such use by the teen-ager who is temporarily deprived of the use of the teen telephone.

In some instances money-earning teen-agers pay for their own telephones. In a few instances revealed in interviews, the parents have provided for the teen telephone in allowances. But, even if parents pay for the total teen telephone charge, according to some parents, the separate teen telephone has reduced family tensions, given the teen-ager a sense of independence, and has assured parental use of a telephone without having to "pull the teen-agers off."

"But we can afford only one telephone," many parents are obliged to say. In this situation there is no alternative to setting time limits on outgoing calls by teen-agers, encouraging them to advise incoming callers of the need to give up the telephone after reasonable conversation, and an agreed-upon signal to interrupt an overlong teen telephone conversation if someone else needs the telephone.

If outgoing or incoming calls connected with parents' work-time responsibilities are heavy, an even more rigid set of guidelines must be formulated for teen use of the telephone—that is, if only one telephone is available in the family. However, if parental use of the telephone is not connected with the work-time responsibilities of either parent, don't be surprised to hear your teen-ager say, "But, Mother . . . Daddy, *you* talked for nearly an hour to *your* friends!" You'd better have a more plausible answer than "I'm paying for the telephone, and I have the right to talk as long as I wish!"

You and I may see it that way, but the teen-ager just doesn't!

10

Resource and Book List

Note: The following list of books, magazines, and other resources is selective, not exhaustive. Choosing between an exhaustive series of lists and a selective list for each division, I have chosen the latter in order to be able to give indications in many instances of the content of books and sections of magazines most helpful. While not necessarily agreeing with everything in some books and articles listed below, I find enough of the helpful to justify the listing, trusting your maturity to discern the wiser philosophies.

Background: Home, Family, Parents

Bell, A. Donald, *The Family In Dialogue,* Grand Rapids, Michigan: Zondervan Press, 1968. This is a helpful volume to parents who are striving to keep good rapport in ideals, plans, cooperation, and discipline.

Brant, Henry H., and Dowdy, Homer H., *Christians Have Troubles, Too,* Old Tappan, New Jersey: Fleming H. Revell, 1969. Written by two eminent Christian psychiatrists who aspire to help readers to find answers in the Bible. Two chapters are particularly relevant:

Chapter 3: *Parents And Children:* Conflict between parents, training and example, the proof of love, consistently firm, squabbling parents, bowing to pressure, a choice of standards, family civil war, acting like a parent, torn between loyalties, etc.

Chapter 4: *Teen-agers:* Self at the center, ashes for beauty, rebellion and witchcraft, tuning out others, too much twosome, education in sex, learning to be truthful, teen-age marriage, mother's baby, skin irritation, tempted to quit, etc.

Thompson, W. Taliaferro, *Adventures In Parenthood,* Richmond, Virginia: John Knox Press, 1959. Although this book is splendid for both fathers and mothers, it is particularly excellent for fathers.

Home Life: A Christian family magazine, published at 127 Ninth Avenue, North, Nashville, Tennessee monthly. This publication is excellent throughout, but may be especially helpful to many families in its monthly departments, "Family Living," and "The Family Teaches."

Parents' Magazine: An excellent general magazine for parents, publhshed by Parents' Magazine Press, 52 Vanderbilt Avenue, New York, N.Y., 10017. Three sections of the magazine are pertinent: "If Your Child Is Under Five Years Of Age," "If Your Child Is Between Five And Ten," "If Your Child Is Between 11 and 18"

Family-Centered Activities

Cleaver, Nancy, *The Treasury Of Family Fun,* Old Tappan, New Jersey: Fleming H. Revell Company, 1960. In keeping with the oft-repeated suggestion that the family which prays together, *plays* together will stay together, this book is what its title implies: a treasure house of happy family activities.

Edwards, Vergne, *The Tired Adult's Guide To Backyard Fun With Kids,* New York, N.Y.: The Association Press, 1965. (291 Broadway, 10017).

Gredd, Elisabeth M., and others, *What To Do When There's Nothing To Do,* New York, N.Y.: The Dell Publishing Company, 1968 (750 Third Avenue, 10017). This book contains many tested play ideas for young children.

Kiester, Edwin, Jr., *How And Where To Vacation With Children And Enjoy It,* Garden City, New York: Doubleday And Company, 1964.

Dealing with Pre-Teens

Chess, Stella . . . Thomas, Alexander . . . Birch, Herbert, *Your Child Is A Person,* New York, N.Y.: Simon and Schuster, Inc., 1964. There are twenty-three meaningful chapters which cover almost every problem which parents face—from "Breast Or Bottle?" to "Establishing Home Rules" to "Sex And Modesty" to "How To Spot Trouble." There are excellent chapters on the "Late Bloomer," "The Handicapped Child," "How To Spot Trouble," and "The Many Ways of Parents."

Edens, David and Virginia, *Why God Gave Children Parents,* Nashville,

Tennessee: Broadman Press, 1966. Written by a husband-wife team who grew up in excellent homes, who have a wide and resourceful background in the area of marriage and the home, and who are excellent parents, teachers, and writers.

Fraiberg, Selma H., *The Magic Years* (Birth to school age), New York, N.Y.: Charles Scribner's Sons, 1959.

Ginott, Haim G., *Between Parent And Child,* New York, N.Y.: The MacMillan Company, 1968. This is one of the most widely read and discussed books of recent years. Candor impels me to say that there are types of permissiveness stated or implied in Dr. Ginott's books in which I do not concur. Yet, there are many excellent insights, and the twelve chapters are well worth the reading.

Homan, William M., M.D., *Child Sense,* New York, N.Y.: Basic Books, Inc., 1969. The ten chapters of this volume justify the prefatory notation that Dr. Homan has "distilled the experiences and knowledge he has gained in over 20 years of practice—observing, advising, and learning from more than 10,000 children." The chapter headings indicate the rich resources of the book: Love, Discipline, Independence, Common Problems With The Young Child, Common Problems Of Older Children, Common Problems Of Family Relationships, Education, Desirable Personality Traits, Sex Education, and the Teaching Of Attitudes, Conclusion.

Hymes, James L. Jr., *Three To Six: Your Child Starts To School,* Public Affairs Pamphlet Number 163, obtainable at 381 Park Avenue, South, New York, N.Y., 10016.

Lambert, Clara, *Understanding Your Child From 6 to 12,* Public Affairs Pamphlet Number 144. Address given immediately above this entry.

Ryan, Bernard, Jr., *Your Child And The First Year Of School,* Cleveland, Ohio: World Publishing Company (2231 West 110 Street), 1969.

Dealing with Teen-agers

Adams, James P., *Understanding Adolescence,* Boston, Mass.: Allyn and Bacon, 1968. In view of the almost-universal difficulty which parents have in remembering the turmoil and confusion of their own years in the teens, reading a book of this type can be most helpful to parents whose children are in their teen years or approaching those years.

Crawford, John and Dorothea, *Better Ways Of Growing Up,* Philadelphia,

Pennsylvania: The Fortress Press, 1964. This book is directed to teen-agers themselves, but can be read to advantage by parents, also. In addition to twelve chapters of such interesting nature as "Growing Up Isn't Easy," "Emotions Must Be Managed," "Self Knowledge Is The Key We Need," "Looking Forward To Marriage," and "Surer Faiths To Live By," there are 17 quizzes, choice lists, and charts for the teen-ager's use.

Duvall, Evelyn Millis, *Keeping Up With Teen-Agers,* Public Affairs Pamphlet Number 177 (381 Park Avenue, South, New York, N.Y.). Concentrated counsel from one of America's wisest counselors on youth problems.

Duvall, Evelyn Millis, *Today's Teenager,* New York, N.Y.: The Association Press, 1966.

Gesell, Arnold . . . Ilg, Frances . . . Ames, Louise, *Youth: The Years From Ten to Sixteen,* New York, N.Y.: Harper and Row, 1966.

Ginott, Haim G., *Between Parent And Teen-Ager,* New York, N.Y.: The MacMillan Company, 1969. As with Dr. Ginott's earlier book, *Between Parent And Child,* I feel that some lines of conviction could have been drawn much more clearly; yet, also, there are some most helpful insights in the twelve chapters.

Landis, Paul K., *Coming Of Age: Problems Of Teen-agers,* Public Affairs Pamphlet Number 234 (381 Park Avenue, South, New York, N.Y., 10016). This pamphlet is directed to the teen-ager, but parents could profit from persuing its topics: "Problems Of Teen Agers," "My Family And I," "Maturing Physically," "Inferiority Feelings," "Manners And Morals," "Your Dating Days."

Menninger, William C., and Others, *How To Understand The Opposite Sex,* New York, N.Y.: Pocketbooks (630 Fifth Avenue), 1964. Eight chapters written by one of America's outstanding Christian psychiatrists and his associates, and filled with tried-and-proved wisdom.

Shedd, Charlie W., *Letters to Karen,* Nashville, Tennessee: Abingdon Press, 1965. Highly popular and widely read, written in diction which appeals to young people, and particularly appropriate to young women approaching marriage.

Shedd, Charlie W., *Letters To Phillip,* Garden City, N.Y.: Doubleday And Company, 1968. Highly acceptable for young men, particularly those who are approaching marriage or are in the early months of marriage.

Sex Instruction

Concordia Press, St. Louis, Missouri, has produced an outstanding Sex Education Series in paperbacks and covering in a truly excellent Christian spirit the needs for sex instruction from childhood to adulthood. Here are the titles:

I Wonder, I Wonder
Wonderfully Made
Take The High Road
Life Can Be Sexual
Parents' Guide To Christian Conversations About Sex
Christian Views Of Sex Education

Duvall, Evelyn Millis and Sylvanus, *Sense And Nonsense About Sex,* New York, N.Y.: The Association Press. Written by a husband and wife team of mature Christians, and supported by many years of study, observation, and counseling of young people.

Duvall, Evelyn Millis, *Why Wait 'Till Marriage?,* New York, N.Y.: The Association Press, 1968 (paperback available). In a day in which the damaging philosophy of "it's only love and not just marriage that gives you the right to each other's body" this clear, intelligent, convincing book is priceless. Any teen-ager who reads this book will *know* that it is important to wait for marriage and will know *why!*

Hymes, James L., *How To Tell Your Child About Sex,* Public Affairs Pamphlet Number 149 (381 Park Avenue, South, New York, N.Y., 10016)

Landers, Ann, *Talks To Teen-agers About Sex,* Englewood Cliffs, New Jersey: Prentice Hall, 1963. With the cleverness of diction and approach which characterizes her columns, this popular writer-counselor "lays the truth on the line" in attractive presentations.

McCoy, Kathy, "How To Say No And Mean It," *Teen Magazine,* May, 1969, pp. 12 ff. An excellent article in teen language concerning a universal problem faced by teen-agers generally, and by teen girls particularly.

Parent And Child Institute, *The Life Cycle Library,* Chicago, Illinois (154 East Erie Street, 60611). This four-volume work is described in Chapter V and is an outstanding aid to parents in Sex instruction. An additional volume, *Parents Answer Book,* comes with the four volumes and contains answers to the 100 questions most frequently asked by children concerning sex.

Shedd, Charlie W., *The Stork Is Dead,* Waco, Texas: WORD BOOKS, 1968. Highly readable, frank and forthright, and most acceptable for giving to teen-agers for their own reading.

Taylor, Kenneth N., *Almost Twelve,* Wheaton, Illinois: Tyndale House. This is a splendidly written story of sex for children.

Help in Special Problems

Discipline:

Chapter 8 of *Child Sense* (William E. Homan), listed under Dealing with Pre-teens

Chapters 2-5 of *Between Parent And Teen-Ager* (Haim Ginott), listed under Dealing with Teen-agers

Chapters 3 and 4 of *Christians Have Troubles Too* (Brant and Dowdy), listed under Background: Home, Family, Parents.

Chapters 10 and 11 of *Your Child Is A Person* (Chase and others), listed under Dealing with Pre-Teens

Baruch, Dorothy, *How To Discipline Your Children,* Public Affairs Pamphlet Number 154 (381 Park Avenue, South, New York, N.Y., 10016).

Beecher, Marguerite and Willard, *Parents On The Run,* New York, N.Y.: Grossett And Dunlap, 1967. This volume is particularly fine in its presentation of the need for discipline, the right and obligation of parents to discipline, and is very aptly called "A common sense book for today's parents."

McLean, Gordon D., *We're Holding Your Son,* Old Tappan, New Jersey: Fleming H. Revell, 1969. This dramatic volume is a factual report of teen-agers from middle class families in our country who have run afoul of the law. It can be helpful to parents of both law-abiding and law-breaking juveniles.

Narramore, Clyde M., *Discipline In The Christian Home,* Grand Rapids, Michigan: Zondervan Press, 1961. This book lists and discusses twenty suggestions for teaching and inculcating discipline in the home.

Drugs, Alcohol, Tobacco:

Drugs:

Federal Source Book: Answers To The Most Frequently Asked Questions About Drug Abuse, Washington, D.C.: Government Printing Office, Department D.

Marshall, Catherine, "An Answer To Drugs," *Guideposts,* May, 1970, pp. 1 ff.

McLean, Gordon F., *High On The Campus,* Wheaton, Illinois: Tyndale Press, 1970. This book is currently being filmed and will appear widely on movie screens throughout our nation, doubtless.

Merke, Donald G., *Drug Abuse: Teenage Hangup,* Dallas, Texas: TANE Press (Texas Alcohol Narcotics Education, 2814 Oak Lawn Avenue, 75219), 1970.

National Association of Blue Shield Plans, *Drug Abuse: The Chemical Cop-Out,* published in April of 1969, available from Blue Shield offices throughout the nation.

Spence, W. R., M.D., *Dial-A-Drug* (Disc And Booklet), obtainable from TANE, 2814 Oak Lawn Avenue, Dallas. (This clever disc is described in Chapter VI and is both eye-catching to youth and immensely helpful.)

TANE (address above) publishes an excellent series of booklets at prices which range currently from 25¢ to 75¢: *Glue Sniffing: Big Trouble In A Tube, Let's Talk About Drugs, Let's Talk About Goof Balls And Pep Pills, LSD; Trip Or Trap? Why Not Marijuana?*

Alcohol:

Curtis, Lindsay R., *Alcohol: Fun Or Folly?,* Dallas, Texas: TANE PRESS, 2814 Oak Lawn Avenue, 75219.

Garmon, William S., *The Many Faces Of Ethyl,* Nashville, Tennessee: Broadman Press, 1966.

Valles, Jorge, M.D., *From Social Drinking To Alcoholism,* Dallas, Texas: TANE Press.

TANE PRESS (Address above) publishes these booklets at the 1970 price of 75¢ each: *Alcohol Or Highway Safety?, Alcohol: Servant Or Master?, Alcohol: Your Blood And Your Brain.*

Teen Magazine, "Life With An Addicted Father," June, 1969, pp. 54-55.

Tobacco:

Cigarette Smoking And Health Characteristics, Public Health Service Publication Number 1000, Series 10, Number 34 (Obtainable from Department of Documents, Government Printing Office, Washington, D.C., the 1970 price being 45¢ per copy).

TANE Press, 2814 Oak Lawn Avenue, Dallas, Texas, publishes these booklets: *Smoking Or Health?*, *Tobacco And Health*, 1970 charges being 60¢ for the former and $1.25 for the latter.

Reading and Movies:

Horn Book Magazine, published six times a year by Horn Book, Inc., 585 Boylston Street, Boston, Mass., 12116. This magazine contains many splendid articles on children's books and literature, excellent book reviews, and announcements and advertisements of new books acceptable for children.

Hurt, Gladys, *Honey For A Child's Heart*, Grand Rapids, Michigan: Zondervan Press, 1969. This volume deals with the imaginative use of books in family life and could turn the frequent monotony of family existence into a happy continuing experience with one's world.

Larrick, Dr. Nancy, *A Parent's Guide To Children's Reading*, Garden City, New York: Doubleday And Company, 1964. This book is particularly helpful to parents of pre-teen children. Its five divisions bear these titles: How You Can Help, Day In and Day Out, How Reading Is Taught Today, Getting the Books He Needs, Books and Magazines for Children, Further Reading for Parents.

Parents' Magazine & Better Family Living, a monthly magazine. Each issue contains "The Family Movie Guide," in which there are appraisals of movies suitable for children 8 to 12, 13 to 17, and 18 and above. There is an original review of reliable nature for each movie in one month's issue, and five successive issues carry a condensation of the appraisal. The P/M Family Medal is awarded to outstanding family films. Special Merit awards are given to superior films of more mature nature. Publisher's address: 52 Vanderbilt Avenue, New York, N.Y., 10017.

Religious Guidance:

Chapter 12 of *Better Ways Of Growing Up* (John and Dorothea Crawford), listed under Dealing with Teen-agers. The chapter is titled "Finding Surer Faith To Live By."

Edens, David and Virginia, *Making The Most Of Family Worship*, Nashville, Tennessee: Broadman Press, 1969. For a family which wishes to begin "family altar" and for families which wish to make this period of family worship more meaningful, this book is helpful.

National Congress Of Parents And Teachers, *In All Good Faiths.* This work deals with religious information which can be shared in the early years of a child's growth, in his elementary school years, and in his adolescent years. There are study-discussion programs and a section titled "Spiritual Soundings."

Neff, Herbert G., *Meaningful Religious Experiences For The Bright And Gifted Child,* New York, N.Y.: The Association Press, 1968.

Thomas Nelson And Sons, Camden, New Jersey, are publishers of a series of youth religious books, some of which have these titles: *Youth Asks: Does God Still Speak?, Youth Considers Doubt And Frustration, Youth Considers "Do It Yourself" Religion, What's Life For?, Youth Asks: Why Bother About God?*

Whitman, Ardis, "What Not To Tell A Child About God," *Reader's Digest,* February, 1962, pp. 81-84.

Parents Without Partners, and *the Working Mother:*

Chapter 19 of *Your Child Is A Person* (Chess, Stella, and others), listed under DEALING WITH PRE-TEENS. The chapter title is "The Working Mother: Not Guilty!"

Egleson, *Parents Without Partners,* New York, N.Y.: Ace Books (1120 Avenue Of The Americas, 10016).

Special Problems With Children:

1. *The Culturally Deprived Child:*
   Crowe, Lester D., and Smythe, Hugh H., and Murray, Walter, *Education For The Culturally Disadvantaged Child,* New York, N.Y.: David McKay, Inc., 1966.

2. *The Gifted Child:*
   Narramore, Clyde M., *Is Your Child Gifted?,* Grand Rapids, Michigan: Zondervan Press.

3. *The Handicapped Child:*
   Chess, Stella . . . Thomas, Alexander . . . Hirch, Herbert, *Your Child Is A Person,* listed under Dealing with Pre-teens, Chapter 21, "The Handicapped Child."

   Wishik, Samuel N., *How To Help Your Handicapped Child,* Public Affairs Pamphlet Number 219 (381 Park Avenue, South, New York, N.Y., 10016)

4. *The "Late Bloomer" Child:*
Chess, Stella, and others, *Your Child Is A Person,* listed under Dealing with Pre-teens, Chapter 20, "The Late Bloomer."

5. *The Shy Child:*
Ross, Helen, *The Shy Child,* Public Affairs Pamphlet Number 239 (381 Park Avenue, South, New York, N.Y. 10016)

6. *The Retarded Child:*
Johnson, G. Orville . . . Kirk, Samuel A., *Educating The Retarded Child,* New York, N.Y.: Houghton Mifflin Company, 1951

Roberts, Nancy, *David,* Richmond, Virginia: John Knox Press, 1968. This is a factual report of intelligent, victorious parental dealing with a retarded child.

7. *Prejudice:*
Clark, Dr. Mamie Phipps, "How To Bring Up Your Child Without Race Prejudice," *Family Circle News,* August, 1968, p. 36 ff. (This magazine is published in Mount Vernon, Illinois, 61054)

Special Note:

For parents who need psychiatrical help for themselves in relation to their children or for the children themselves may find this reference helpful:

Ginott, Haim, *Between Parent And Child,* listed under Dealing with Pre-teens:
Chapter 11: "Children In Need Of Professional Help."
Chapter 12: "Parents In Need Of Professional Help."

Findings of Parent-Youth Survey

Note: The portions of my survey of parents and teen-agers shared in Chapter I are not repeated here. Those portions listed POINTS OF TENSION between parents and teen-agers (as reported by both parents and teen-agers), EFFECTIVE DISCIPLINARY TECHNIQUES (as viewed by both parents and teen-agers), and teen-agers' suggestions concerning what parents could do to help them face their problems that they are not now doing. The following findings constitute the remainder of the survey.

As the Teen-agers See It

List the problems of people your age that worry you most.

1. Compromise of principle to achieve popularity
2. Loose sex standards
3. Drinking
4. Lack of communication with parents
5. (Tie): Drugs
        Too early dating, too early marriage
6. Concern for college entrance to preferred college.
7. Vocational choice
8. (Tie): Lack of concern for religion
        Lack of respect for nation, God, parents.

(In this, as in all other instances in the survey, more items were listed than those lists indicate; yet, the items in the lists given here were mentioned the largest number of times)

Rate these problems in order of their seriousness in your community (Number 1, most serious, Number 2, next most serious, etc.).

Here are the ratings given by those involved in the survey:

1. Liquor
2. Vulgar speech
3. Pre-marital sex
4. Dishonesty

5. Narcotics
6. (Tie): Obscene literature
   Too-early steady dating
7. Necking–petting

What could your church do to help youth to face and handle today's youth problems (that it is not now doing)?

1. The largest number of replies brought this thrilling report: "Our church is doing everything young people need from the church" (They listed guest speakers, films, panels, books, trips to publicly supported institutions for rehabilitation, retreats, fellowship, and personal counseling).
2. More "talk-outs" and "talk-backs."
3. More youth counselors, preferably nearer our age (college-career young people were mentioned repeatedly)
4. A more practical relating of Christian principles to problems of our daily lives in Bible teaching, preaching, and youth activities.
5. More youth participation in church activities and decisions through hearing with respect the advice of youth councils.
6. (Tie): More youth outreach through guided activities beyond the church buildings (witnessing, ministering to human need in the area generally)
   More involvement of youth in the full program of the church.

What could your school do to help to meet today's pressures?

1. Develop and maintain a better sense of values (avoid excessive grade pressure, emphasize character values more, don't concentrate "heroes" exclusively to outstanding athletes, realize that the whole personality of the student needs to be developed).
2. Provide for more personal attention in both teaching and counseling.
3. Require more maturity and skill on the part of teachers.
4. (Tie): More student participation in determining courses, teachers, student activities.

More outside speakers who can help students in decisions.
More teachers with high levels of understanding and communication.
5. More safe information on sex and drugs.

From what sources have you received most help in understanding and handling your personal problems? (The following are listed in order of frequency mentioned):

1. From the church (pastor, staff, teachers, counselors, special weeks, youth programs, wholesome friends)
2. From my parents
3. From Christian friends (some my age, some older)
4. From school (teachers, counselors, films, activities)
5. From personal religious sources (Prayer, God's Word, meditation, reading, living).
6. From my peers (people my age whose spiritual strength I respected)

As the Adults See It

What are your greatest concerns for young people of our day?
1. Disrespect for law and order
2. Lack of concern for God, Bible, Prayer, church.
3. Drugs, liquor, sex
4. Lack of self-discipline
5. Poor sense of values
6. (Tie): Pressure of their peers
        Irresponsibility
        Lack of wholesome influence
7. Apathy (apparent lack of motivation)
8. "Rebellion without a cause."
9. Effect of liberal teaching upon their conduct
10. Inability of adult leadership to communicate reasons.

What more do you feel our churches can do to help both parents and their teen-agers to understand and handle problems of today?
1. More literature and program personnel relevant to today's problems (films, doctors, judges, etc.)

2. More family-related activities (parents and teen-agers in the same groups for discussions with pastor, doctor, family counselor, etc., even some meetings in locations outside the church building).
3. Training groups for adults designed to give them better insight to youth problems and techniques of handling them.
4. Bible-centered, but more relevant preaching and teaching.
5. More "outreach" activities for youth.
6. (Tie): More youth Bible study groups with emphasis upon school and community problems

    Better trained Sunday School teachers.
7. (Tie): More church counseling

    Greater use of people under 21 on committees.

    More church-directed education in problems of sex and drug abuse.

What more do you feel that our schools can do in this regard?

1. Maintain better-balanced values (e.g., decrease of social and athletic emphasis, decreasing in some instances the overattention to the "brains" in the student body, increasing emphasis upon patriotism, respect for law and the rights of others.
2. More intelligent, relevant education in liquor, tobacco, sex, and drugs.
3. Better discipline (strict, but consistent; less corporate and more individual; more student participation in setting and maintaining conduct standards).
4. More parental involvement through parents leagues and parent-student cooperation.
5. More mature, morally strong teachers.
6. (Tie): More and better counseling

    Bible student and prayer opportunities available on a voluntary basis.

Notes

Chapter Two
[1] Robert H. Lauer, "Teach Your Child To Say No," *Home Life,* August, 1967, p. 38.
[2] *Ibid.,* pp. 38-39.

Chapter Three
[1] *New York Times,* January 12, 1967.
[2] *The Dallas Morning News,* June 21, 1968.
[3] *Family Weekly,* November 16, 1969, p. 6.
[4] From *Phoenix* (Arizona) *Gazette.*
[5] *NEA Dispatch,* January 5, 1962.

Chapter Four
[1] Richard Cabot, *Honesty* (New York: McMillan, 1966).
[2] *Family Weekly,* June 14, 1970, p. 14.
[3] *Guideposts,* July, 1970, pp. 1-2. Used by permission of Walter Cronkite.
[4] "Dear Abby," from *Fort Worth Star-Telegram,* August 29, 1969.

Chapter Five
[1] *Parents Magazine,* April, 1969, p. 40.
[2] *Christian Life,* June, 1968, for the article, "How To Organize A Sex Education Program In The Church," p. 36.
[3] Reported in "Youth Notes" section of *Parade Magazine,* July 5, 1970, p. 7.
[4] Your author read the series in *Lubbock* (Texas) *Avalanche-Journal,* beginning June 5, 1967. The series was a reprint from *The Minneapolis Tribune,* carrying by-line of Irv Letofsky.
[5] The wording is from the introductory brochure of *The Life Cycle Library.* Information concerning series and publisher in book list.

Chapter Six
[1] Bernard H. Gould, *National Enquirer,* June ___, 1970, p. 6.
[2] Donald J. Merki, *Drug Abuse: Teen-age Hangup,* p. 69.
[3] *Ibid.,* p. 25.

[4] Cartoon by LePelley in *The Christian Science Monitor.*
[5] *A Federal Source Book,* p. 2.
[6] Donald J. Merki, *op. cit.,* pp. 23-24.
[7] *A Federal Source Book,* p. 6.
[8] Jon Phelps, *Durham Herald* (North Carolina).
[9] *Teen Magazine,* June, 1969, pp. 72 ff.

Chapter Seven
[1] *National Enquirer,* July 10, 1970.
[2] *Ibid.*
[3] *Parade Magazine,* May 24, 1970.
[4] *Ibid.,* July, 14, 1963.
[5] *Ibid.*
[6] *Ibid.*
[7] *Home Life,* 127 Ninth Avenue, North, Nashville, Tenn. (Dr. Edens is Director of Marriage and Family Programs, Stephens College)
[8] Lloyd Shearer, *Parade Magazine,* July 14, 1963.
[9] See resource-book list at conclusion of this volume.
[10] *Reader's Digest,* September 1967, pp. 157-62.
[11] Full brochure obtainable upon request: Christian Life Commission, Baptist Building, Dallas, Texas.
[12] See resource book list in the last chapter of this volume.
[13] William Homan, *Child Sense.* (See resource-book list.)

Chapter Eight
[1] *Christian Herald,* February, 1968, p. 21.
[2] *Ibid.,* pp. 18-19.
[3] Arlie B. Davidson, "Everybody Needs Affection," *Montgomery Advertiser,* July, 1970.